Here is what people say about the seminar upon which this book is based:

'Brilliant. Very glad I did it. A fantastic and worthwhile course.'

'Great presentation. Opened my eyes to how to achieve my goals.'

'I found this to be a really inspiring day, specifically hearing about real-life stories.'

'Excellent. Helped me a lot – was truly inspirational.'

'Thoroughly enjoyed it and will recommend it.'

'A very useful and informative presentation that I am very glad I had the good fortune to experience.'

'It was a real eye-opener to look upon my goals completely differently.'

'Very inspirational. Stories were particularly inspiring.'

'A unique, riveting and enlightening course.'

'A very interesting day. Well worth it. Made me think of what I want out of my life.'

D0332888

Adam Walker is a leading authority on personal effectiveness. During the past 16 years his seminars have helped many thousands of people to make lasting changes in their lives and several hundred companies to achieve a significant increase in their profitability. He is also Chairman of the Adam Walker Foundation, a not-for-profit organisation that shows young people how to achieve more from their lives by setting measurable goals for the future.

WHEN
SUCCESS
IS NOT
ENOUGH

ADAM WALKER

PIATKUS

Visit the Piatkus website!

Piatkus publishes a wide range of best-selling fiction and non-fiction, including books on health, mind, body & spirit, sex, self-help, cookery, biography and the paranormal.

If you want to:
- read descriptions of our popular titles
- buy our books over the internet
- take advantage of our special offers
- enter our monthly comp~~etition~~
- learn more about your

VISIT OUR WEBSITE AT:

Copyright © 2004 by Adam Walker

First published in 2004 by
Piatkus Books Limited
5 Windmill Street
London WIT 2JA
e-mail: info@piatkus.co.uk

The moral right of the author has been asserted

A catalogue record for this book is available from the British Library

ISBN 0 7499 2553 1

This book has been printed on paper manufactured with respect for the environment using wood from managed sustainable resources

Edited by Lizzie Hutchins
Text design by Paul Saunders

Typeset by Palimpsest Book Production Limited, Polmont, Stirlingshire
Printed and bound in Great Britain by Clowes Ltd, Beccles, Suffolk

Contents

Acknowledgements

This book would not have been possible without the help of a great many people. In particular I would like to thank:

- The many authors and speakers who have inspired me to set out and continue on my own journey of self-discovery.

- The thousands of delegates at my seminars who have helped me to test, refine and develop this material over the last 16 years.

- My researcher Barbara James for her tenacity and attention to detail in checking all my facts.

- My PA Lyn Harding for her hard work in preparing the many drafts of the manuscript.

- My wife Kym for allowing me to use her story as an example of goal-setting.

- Franklyn Covey for giving permission to use their mission-statement sequence.

- Richard Bandler for giving permission to use his sub-modalities check list.

- My literary agent Euan Thorneycroft of Curtis Brown for helping to turn an idea into a reality.

- My editor, Penny Phillips, and all the other staff at my publishers, Piatkus, for their help in producing the finished book.

Introduction

Before you start reading this book you need to make an important decision: you need to decide how much benefit you want to get from it.

If you want to get just a little bit of value from it, then read it like a novel and enjoy it. However, if you really want to get the very most from this book, you will need to *do* it, not just read it. This means taking a decision now to complete all the exercises, even those that may seem a little odd to you on first reading. In order to do this you will need a pen and a notebook in which to keep a record of all your answers. If you do this, you will, I promise, get 100 times more value from this book.

I do hope that you will enjoy the book and get lasting benefit from it.

Adam Walker
February 2004

A successful person is someone who has a satisfactory present, a fully resolved past and a compelling, exciting and purpose-driven future.

PART ONE

———

Knowing what
you really want

CHAPTER 1

What is success?

We all want to be successful, but what is success?

Success means different things to different people. So what does it mean to you? Before you read any further, take a moment to answer these two questions:

- What does success mean to me?

- How will I know when I have become successful?

I open my seminars by asking my audiences to answer these two questions and I am constantly amazed by the variety of answers that I get. Some people equate success solely with financial success. Some talk of the career that they would like to have. Some talk about finding someone to love. Some talk about improving their health or their physical appearance. The variety of answers is simply enormous.

And so it should be. Everyone is different. There are no right or wrong answers to these questions (although some answers are more likely to bring happiness and fulfilment than others). However, by far the most common answer is: 'I don't really know.'

And therein lies the problem. Society puts us under the most intense pressure to be successful, without adequately defining what 'success' really is. The result for so many people is a lifetime spent chasing the end of a rainbow, a lifetime of telling themselves that when they have achieved this or bought that *then* they will at last be happy. But the promised happiness never comes. There always seems to be one last condition that must be met before the elusive goal of true happiness and fulfilment can be enjoyed.

So what *is* success?

Before I give you my answer, please do two more things for me:

● Write down the names of three successful people whom you admire. (They can be world leaders, people from history, politicians past or present, business leaders, sportsmen or -women or just ordinary people you know and admire.)

● What do you most admire about these people? Write it down.

I ask delegates at my seminars to do this exercise too and this time I am fascinated by how *similar* their answers are. The same names come up time and time again – world leaders such as:

● Winston Churchill
● Nelson Mandela
● Mahatma Gandhi

business leaders such as:

● Richard Branson
● Bill Gates
● Sir John Harvey Jones

and sportsmen and -women such as:

● David Beckham
● Ellen MacArthur
● Michael Schumacher

So what do all these people have in common? Well, to my mind it's this:

a sense of purpose

The one thing that all these people share is a burning sense of purpose, a vision for the future so strong that it inspired them to achieve the impossible.

David Beckham wanted to be a footballer from the very earliest moment that he can remember. Ellen MacArthur famously saved up her school dinner money to buy her first boat. Their burning sense of purpose drove them to become extraordinary. It gave them their passion to reach the very top of their chosen fields and it continues to drive them every day of their lives to achieve new peaks of excellence. These are the sort of people whom I most admire: people who are living their purpose.

Very few people have such a strong sense of purpose, but by God you will know them when you meet them. They live more, care more, achieve more, love more and enjoy more than other people. They light up other people's lives like a ray of sunshine on a winter's day.

So what does this have to do with you? Well, let me make that connection right now. The power of purpose isn't something that benefits only famous people – it's something that can transform the quality of *anybody's* life.

People who have a sense of purpose come from all walks of life. Many are neither rich nor famous, but they still have the power to touch the lives of everyone they meet. And you can too.

Anyone can discover their sense of purpose at any time in their lives. I'll show you how to go about discovering yours, but before I do, let me a take a moment to tell you about some of the people like this whom I have met recently.

The first is a man called Pete Egoscue, whom I met on a course in Hawaii. Pete is a former US Marine who was shot and seriously wounded in Vietnam. Doctors told him that his injuries were so severe that he would never walk properly again. But Pete refused to accept this. In an attempt to overcome his injuries he bought himself a pile of books on anatomy and yoga and designed his own regime of exercises. To the astonishment of his doctors, he not only taught himself to walk again, but became fit enough to rejoin the Marines as a serving officer!

Word of Pete's remarkable recovery quickly spread and other injured servicemen started to come to him for advice. He shared his exercises with them, with excellent results, and his reputation soon spread far beyond the military community. Today he runs a clinic in San Diego, California, that treats thousands of patients with back pain, arthritis and sports injuries each year.

The Egoscue Clinic has an international reputation for excellence in its field and its success has made Pete a wealthy man. But financial success is not what I admire him for. What I admire most about Pete is his burning sense of purpose. Despite his wealth, he continues to treat patients on a daily basis and he obviously loves his work as much now as he did the day he started.

I watched him treat a man in his early fifties who had been in pain from an ankle injury for 15 years. The patient had tried everything – surgery, painkillers, massage – but nothing had worked. Pete got him free from pain in 15 minutes and gave him a regime of exercises to deal with the pain permanently. The man was so grateful that he literally had tears in his eyes – he couldn't believe he was free of pain for the first time in all those years! I saw the look on Pete's face as he finished the treatment and I knew that here was a man who was living his purpose. If he lives to be 100, Pete Egoscue will probably spend his last day in that clinic saying, 'Just a moment, God, I just need to finish treating this one last patient before I go.' That's what I call success – a man who is living his purpose.

From the field of music someone I admired enormously was the saxophone player Dick Morrissey. He was a jazz saxophonist and session musician who played on literally hundreds of records in the 1970s, '80s and early '90s. I saw him play live with his band Morrissey Mullin on many occasions. As soon as he came on stage you just knew that this was a man who loved being a musician.

Sadly, Dick Morrissey died on 8 November 2000 from cancer of the spine, one of the most cruel and painful cancers of them all. But despite being in severe pain and confined to a wheelchair for the last year of his life, he carried on playing right up to the very end. In fact he played his last concert just a few days before he died. By this time he was bedridden, but that didn't stop him. He got some friends to carry his bed down the high street to his local pub in Deal, Kent, so that he could play one last gig. What a way to go!

The people I've described so far are all people who have already reached the top in their chosen field. But the same sense of purpose can transform anyone's life, even that of someone who is not 'successful' in conventional terms. Let me demonstrate this by telling you about two more people I have met recently.

The first is a girl called Heather whom I met on holiday one year. Heather is not rich or famous and she may never be, but her energy, vivacity and joy for life are powerful enough to light up anyone's day. And where does this energy come from? It comes from a love for the work that she does. Heather is a dolphin trainer. She told me that she had wanted to work with dolphins since she was six years old. It took her 16 years to realise her dream, but when you watch her at work you can see that it was worth the wait. Heather is another wonderful example of someone who has found real fulfilment from living her purpose.

The last person I would like to tell you about is a teacher called Jeff whom I met at a summer camp for young people that I attended in Nevada. Jeff has not always worked as a teacher. For 20 years he worked as a building contractor. He had always wanted to be a teacher, but his dad was a teacher and Jeff didn't get on with him, so he decided to choose another profession.

Jeff spent 20 years building a 'successful' business, but the desire to teach never left him. Finally, at the age of 40, he found that the urge to teach became irresistible. Jeff sold his construction business and went back to college to study for his teaching qualifications. His family had to make huge financial sacrifices to support him. But they recognised how important his career move was to him and were happy to do so.

Jeff came out of college with excellent grades and could have got a job anywhere. He chose, however, to take a job in one of the toughest schools in America. In one class of 38, only six students had both parents still living at home. The students' lives are constantly touched by poverty, drugs and violence. The first job many mornings is to get the first-aid box out to patch up someone who has been beaten up by their peers, or even by their own parents.

In conventional terms Jeff's achievements are modest – it is beyond his power to reach some of his pupils and many still leave school without formal qualifications. However, Jeff focuses on those he *can* help, not those he can't, and his eyes light up when he tells stories about all the times when he has been able to make a difference. It would be hard to find a better example of someone who gains fulfilment from living their purpose.

These are the sort of people whom I most admire. To my mind they are successful in the truest sense of the word because they have a vision for their lives. That vision gives them their charisma, their joy, their purpose and their passion, and from that passion comes their success and their fulfilment. That's my definition of success.

It is my belief that a person's level of happiness and fulfilment is in direct proportion to their strength of purpose. This can be arranged as a hierarchy:

1. At the very bottom is the person with nothing to do and nowhere to go. They might spend much of their time slumped on the sofa switching aimlessly between TV channels or wandering pointlessly through the shopping centre looking at things they are never going to buy. Such people have little or nothing to occupy their present and nothing to look forward to in their future.

2. At the next level is the person who is running for a bus. During those few moments of the chase they have no time to consider the future because their entire focus is on the present moment.

3. At the third level is the person who is looking forward to something that will happen later the same day. What they are doing in the present may or may not be satisfying to them, but if it is

not, their boredom is mitigated by the anticipation of pleasure later.

4. At the fourth level is the person who is involved in planning something important or exciting that is due to take place in a week or two's time – a huge party perhaps, or a job interview, or the purchase of a new car. Their anticipation of the final event gives them a temporary purpose and they will derive further pleasure from completing some of the interim tasks along the way.

5. At the fifth level is the person who is giving their all to achieving something wonderful in a year or two's time – a new career perhaps, or starting a business, or getting married, or having their first child. Whatever it is, it is something that they want so badly that they can feel themselves growing as a person as they overcome the challenges that they meet along the way. This is how most happy and successful people live, moving from one challenge to the next. But there is another level above this.

6. At the very top of my hierarchy of purpose are people like Pete Egoscue, Dick Morrissey, Heather and Jeff – people who have a lifelong sense of purpose, people who feel that they are on a mission, a mission so strong that it inspires them to become extraordinary. These are the people I most admire.

So what's your purpose? Well, don't worry if you haven't discovered it yet. Not everyone is born knowing what they came here to do. A sense of purpose is something that can be discovered at any time of life and some people find it later than others. Perhaps the greatest example of this is the failed politician who by the age of 65 had spent many years on the back benches. His name was Winston Churchill.

It's never too late to discover your sense of purpose. It might take you a while to find it, but you'll know when you have because, unlike the quest for material success, it will give you a deep sense of fulfilment at every stage along the way. It will inspire you to achieve the impossible and give you the determination to overcome the obstacles that you are sure to encounter. It may also bring you material success, but by the time it does so, you may find that this has become less important to you. In fact a very convenient way to measure your strength of purpose is to ask yourself, 'Would I carry on doing this if I didn't have to?' If you can answer 'yes', then you have found your purpose. If not, then you need to read the next chapter.

CHAPTER 2

How to discover what you really want

The need to have a vision or a sense of purpose is not my idea. It's referred to throughout history. In Greek mythology, in philosophy and in the Bible, time after time references are made to the power of purpose, yet only a tiny percentage of people have a vision for their lives. The vast majority float along like pieces of driftwood in a river, their course altered by every rock, eddy and current that they encounter, just hoping forlornly that they will like the place they end up in and will have a few nice experiences along the way.

So what's your purpose? What's your passion? What's your vision for the future?

You might well be thinking, 'I don't know.' Well, don't worry, that's quite usual. I'm going to spend the rest of this chapter taking you through a process that will help you to find your purpose. Before I do so, just take a few moments to complete another exercise.

Write down in your notebook a list of all the things that you *don't* want in your future life, for example:

- I don't want to be poor.

- I don't want to be lonely.

- I don't want to be unhappy.

You might well find that what you *do* want is the exact opposite of what you don't want, so a good way to start finding out what you want might be to write down the antithesis of the list you have just compiled.

But most people never get round to doing this. What they do instead is to keep focusing on what they *don't* want. Let me give you an example of how dangerous this is.

- Stand up and put your feet close together so that they actually touch.

- Put your arms down by your sides.

- Now imagine that you are standing on the very edge of a high cliff with the wind howling around your ears. Imagine that you are hundreds of feet above the sea and that the waves are pounding on the rocks below.

- Imagine what would happen if you lost your balance and fell over the edge. Your body would certainly be torn to pieces on the rocks below.

- Now I'd like you to close your eyes and focus your whole attention on *not* wobbling. Keep your eyes shut for one whole minute and just keep saying to yourself over and over again, 'Don't wobble.' Focus your whole attention on what would happen if you fell over the edge and just keep saying to yourself out loud, 'Don't wobble, don't wobble, don't wobble.'

This is another exercise that I do at my seminars and I often have to cut it short because people start wobbling so much that I worry that they might fall over and hurt themselves!

So why does this happen? Well, the reason is that your sense of balance is controlled by your subconscious mind, not your conscious mind. Psychologists tell us that the subconscious mind is approximately 30,000 times more powerful than the conscious mind. It controls almost everything that we do. It controls our breathing, our heartbeat, our balance and it controls and processes our thoughts. In any battle between the conscious and the sub-conscious mind, the subconscious will always win.

Let me prove this to you. I would like you to instruct your conscious mind *not* to think of elephants. Now I said, *'Don't* think of elephants.' Please banish them from your thoughts immediately. Don't think about elephants. Now what are you thinking about right now? Does it have four legs and a trunk?

As I said, in any battle between the conscious mind and the subconscious mind, the subconscious mind will always win. And this is a great metaphor for life. If you try not to think of elephants, you start to think of nothing else. If you focus on not wobbling, you wobble so much that you nearly fall over. So what do you think might happen if you focus on *not* being fat, or *not* being poor, or *not* being lonely?

Focus on what you do want

So what can you do to keep your subconscious mind on track? What can you do to achieve more of the things that you want to achieve? Well, it's very simple. All you need to do is to focus on what you *do* want rather than what you *don't* want. That's what successful people do.

Sounds simple, doesn't it? But exactly how do you go about doing it? I'm going to take you through an exercise right now that will help you to get started. It's one of the most important exercises in this book. In order for you to get the most out of it I'd like to suggest that you read through it in its entirety before actually doing it.

YOUR BIRTHDAY PARTY

Once you have read through all the instructions below, I'd like you to stand up and close your eyes. (It's important to close your eyes because doing so will shut out the distractions of your surroundings.)

- With your eyes closed, I'd like you to imagine that you are in a glass time capsule that can take you many years into the future. I'd like you to imagine that you are travelling through time, through tomorrow, through next week, through next year and on and on through time until you reach a time ten years from now.

- It's your birthday and you are having a birthday party. It's a huge event and everyone you know is there. All the people who matter most in your life have gathered to celebrate your life so far. Look around the room. Who do you see? Your wife or husband or partner perhaps? Your parents, your children, your brothers and sisters? Your friends, your colleagues from work?

- Each of these people is going to make a speech about your life and about your achievements. Think carefully about what you would like each person to say about you.

- Start with someone associated with your work. Who is it? Who do you see? Is it your boss, a colleague, an employee or a satisfied customer? Get a picture of someone clearly in your mind. Now what would you like this person to say about your career? How did you spend it? What job did you choose? Where did you end up? What achievements are you most proud of? How do you feel about all your career achievements? What would you like this person to say about you? You are going to write all this down in a few moments' time, so be sure that you have an image of someone very clearly in your mind.

- Your partner is going to be the next person to speak. If you are already in a committed relationship, get a picture clearly in your mind of your partner as they will look in ten years' time. If not, then get a picture in your mind of your ideal partner. What do they look like? How do you feel when you look at them?

- Now what would you like your partner to say about your relationship? What would you like them to say about your life together, about the experiences that you have shared? How did you show them your love? What achievements are you most proud of? What experiences did you enjoy most? How would you like to feel about your relationship? You are going to write down what your partner is saying in a moment, so focus clearly on what they are saying about you.

- The third person to speak is your best friend. Get a picture clearly in your mind of your best friend as they will be in ten years' time or of the sort of person you would like to have as your best friend.

- Now what would you like them to say about you? What would you like them to say about your friendship? How did you serve them as a friend? What sort of friend would you like to have been? You are going to write down what they are saying about you in a moment's time, so get an image clearly in your mind.

- The final person who is going to speak is your mother, father or guardian. Get a picture clearly in your mind of your mother, father or guardian as they will be in ten years' time. If your parents are no longer alive, recall instead an image from a favourite photograph or just think of them as you would like to remember them.

- Now what would you like your mother or father to say at that birthday party? Don't think about what they have said to you in the past. Focus instead on what you would really like them to say. What would you like them to say about the way that your life has turned out? What have you done to make them proud of you? How would it feel to know that your parents were so proud of your achievements? Which of your many successes are they focusing on now? How does it feel to hear such a positive tribute to your life so far?

- The best way to do this exercise is to take each person in turn. Close your eyes (this really is important) and spend at least two minutes thinking about what you would like your boss or work colleague to say about you. You might like to have some music playing quietly while you do it. Once you have spent at least two minutes with your eyes closed, focusing on what this person is saying about you, open your eyes and spend at least two more minutes writing it all down. If you can't think what to write, trust your instincts and write the very first thing that comes into your head, using the power of your subconscious mind.

- Once you are sure that you have everything down, move on to your partner. Spend at least another two minutes with your eyes closed, focusing on your partner and what you would really like to hear them say about you – not what you think they might say, but what you would really like them to say.

- Do the same thing again with your best friend's tribute.

- Finish off by writing down what you would like your mother, father or guardian to say in celebration of your achievements during these ten years.

It might take half an hour or more to do this exercise, but if you do it properly and with real emotion I promise that you will find it very powerful. If you don't have half an hour to spend right now, I suggest that you put this book down and return to it when you do.

I am assuming that you have now completed the birthday party exercise. Well done. A lot of people find that exercise to be quite emotional – it has some in tears – but most people find it to be hugely valuable. It's only when you have a clear idea of where you want to end up that you can start the process of planning how you are going to get there. Without a clear sense of purpose and direction it is so very easy to spend a lifetime clawing your way up the ladder of success only to find when you get to the very top that it was leaning against completely the wrong wall. What a tragedy that would be.

Who is controlling you?

Most delegates of my live seminars get powerful insights from the birthday party exercise, but not everyone enjoys it.

I'll never forget an incident that occurred at a seminar that I gave in the Midlands in 1998. I had just finished explaining this topic when a tall, distinguished-looking man in his early fifties put his hand up.

'Do you have a question?' I asked.

'Well, it's not exactly a question,' he replied, 'but I'd like to tell you that no one tells me how to live my life, I just take each day as it comes and see what life brings. I think this goal-setting business is a load of complete mumbo-jumbo.'

When you speak to as many people as I do each year, you expect to meet the odd person like this. I certainly don't take such comments personally, so I thanked the chap for his input, pointed out that most other people in the room had found the topic useful and said that I hoped that he would enjoy some of the other topics later in the seminar.

It was a two-day programme and the following morning no sooner had I stood up than the same chap put his hand up again.

'Do you have a question?' I asked.

'Well,' he said, 'it's not exactly a question...'

Here we go again, I thought.

'I just wanted to tell you,' he continued, 'that I went home last night and told my wife what we had been doing today. I told her that I thought that this goal-setting business was a load of complete mumbo-jumbo. Without a word she went upstairs and returned with a big thick hard-backed notebook. On the front cover it said "Christine's Goal Book". Inside were pages and pages of goals. Quite unbeknown to me, she's been writing down her goals for years.'

This part of his story was funny enough, but what he told us next had the whole audience shaking with laughter.

'As I read through her book I could hardly believe what I saw there. Everything that we've achieved together, everything we've ever talked about, all our major decisions were written down in that book. Last year's holiday in Venice, having our third child, building the extension, having her parents come to live with us – all the things that I thought were my idea were written down in that book. It's obvious that she has been controlling my life for years!'

This is why goal-setting is so important. You might not have a plan for your life, but you can be absolutely sure that someone else has one for you! It could be anyone. It might be your partner. It might be a parent who decides that you should take this job or marry that person. It may be peer pressure that influences what you do with your life. Worst of all, it may be advertisers or the media who spend hundred of millions of pounds each year trying to convince us all that the key to happiness is to buy this car, this watch or that pair of jeans. If you don't take the time to discover your own sense of purpose, you will be like a gigantic vacuum waiting to suck in every idea that passes by. You simply must find your sense of purpose before someone else imposes theirs upon you!

Many people discover their sense of purpose through completing my 'birthday party' exercise. If you have discovered yours then I suggest that you put this book down now and go out and celebrate. You have just made a discovery that will change the course of your life.

If you haven't yet found your sense of purpose, don't worry. You can repeat this exercise again whenever you like and you will gain new insights each time you do so. You may have a breakthrough in a few minutes' time. It may come to you in the bath next month. Alternatively, you may discover a medium-term purpose, for example getting a new job, which serves as a stepping-stone to discovering your ultimate purpose.

Some people find it harder to detect their sense of purpose than others. However, what I do know is that if you keep on asking the right questions you will ultimately be successful. It's just a matter of patience and persistence.

But even if the last exercise did help you to discover your sense of purpose, the images that were conjured up will be rather vague and distant. What you need now to guide you through your day to day life are some concrete goals, and this is exactly what we are going to look at in the next chapter.

CHAPTER 3

How to set goals that really inspire you

Whenever I talk about goal-setting to business audiences, people come up to me afterwards and ask me the same question: 'Why on earth weren't we taught this at school?'

In order to address this issue I set up a separate not-for-profit organisation, the Adam Walker Foundation, in June 2001, and I now spend part of my time presenting seminars on goal-setting to teenage audiences. My school seminars are the most demanding seminars that I run – teenagers are not slow to tell you if they are not enjoying something. However, they are also the most satisfying. So many of my business delegates have spent 10, 20 or even 30 years climbing the ladder of success only to find it was leaning against entirely the wrong wall; it's a real privilege to have an opportunity to teach goal-setting to people who have their whole lives ahead of them.

I always start my school seminars in the same way. I ask people to stand up if they have at least one goal that they would like to achieve in the future. Almost everyone stands up. Then I ask them to stay standing if they have written that goal down anywhere. Typically 75 per cent of them sit down. Then I ask those still standing to remain standing if they read their goals at least once a day. Almost everyone sits down. If anyone is still standing, I ask them if they have their goals with them. Fewer than one person in 1,000 can show them to me.

I then go on to tell the story of how I became interested in goal-setting. I was 22 and until then I had no goals for my life at all. I just drifted along and took each day as it came. As a result I lost all interest in my schoolwork and ended up in a dead-end job earning a pittance and living in a horrid damp rented cottage. I had a pretty negative attitude to life and I used to spend a lot of my time bitching about people who had more than I did. 'It's all right for him,' I used to think to myself as someone drove by in an expensive sports car, 'he must have had it all handed to him on a plate.' Success of any sort had eluded me. I was thoroughly disillusioned with my life and full of frustration, anger and resentment. Then, as if I wasn't feeling bad enough already, my girlfriend left me (with hindsight I don't blame her). I fell into a black pit of despair. I stopped going out. I let the washing-up pile up around me. I just felt that the whole world was against me. I was at rock bottom.

But someone up there must have been watching out for me. One day, after a month or so of wallowing in self-pity, I went out to buy a sandwich. Next to the sandwich shop was a second-hand bookshop. Outside the bookshop was a table full of books and right on top of one of the piles was a bright yellow book entitled *How to Get What You Want Out of Life*. On impulse I paid 20p for it.

As soon as I started reading it I knew that the book had been written especially for me. In one of the very first chapters there was a story about a survey that was carried out in 1953 at Yale University, one of the best universities in the United States. A researcher was commissioned to ask the graduate class of 1953 what plans they had for their future lives. One of the questions that the graduates were asked was: 'Do you have any written goals for the future?' Despite the fact that the students were amongst the brightest and most privileged students in America, only 4 per cent had written goals.

Twenty years later the researcher was commissioned to track down the surviving members of the class to find out what they had made of their lives. To his astonishment, he found that those who had written down their goals 20 years previously were on average 30 times richer than those who had not. In fact the net worth of the 4 per cent with written goals exceeded the net worth of the 96 per cent without them. Just as importantly, though, the 4 per cent with written goals seemed happier in other, non-material ways. They reported better health, better-quality relationships and a greater sense of fulfilment than those who had not written down their goals.

I was mesmerised by this story. I took the next day off work and spent the entire day writing down everything that I wanted to achieve in my life. I was suddenly fired with an enthusiasm that I'd never known before. I wrote pages and pages about my goals, my hopes and my dreams for the future, including some huge dreams that at the time seemed absolutely impossible to achieve.

And do you know what? As if by magic, they started to come true. I left the horrid damp cottage, I got a new and much better job and I paid off all my debts. Six years later I had achieved every single thing that I'd put down on that list:

- I had met and married my wife.
- I had bought a beautiful home.
- I had achieved financial security.
- I had found a career that I adored.

Setting goals transformed my life, but for years I used to regret the years that I wasted between the ages of 16 and 22 when I was drifting through life without any goals, purpose or passion. These days I don't regret losing those six years quite so much, because I realise that they provided me with the contrast that enables me to appreciate all the wonderful things that I have in my life now. But part of me would still like to have those years back to live again.

But I count myself lucky because at least I discovered my sense of purpose when I was 22. I often meet people in their forties, fifties or even sixties who have spent an entire lifetime floating along hoping they will like what tomorrow brings or, worse still, have become 'successful', only to find that they aren't getting the fulfilment that they expected from their success. That's why I set up the Adam Walker Foundation: to introduce people to the concept of goal-setting *before* they spend 20 years climbing the wrong ladder. Introducing the concept of setting written goals to the other 96 per cent of the population is my passion and I shall not rest until goal-setting becomes a subject that is taught as universally as reading and writing.

Setting your goals

So let's look now at how you can set goals for your life that will not only inspire you but also bring you a deep sense of satisfaction and fulfilment. The key to achieving this is to maintain a proper balance between the different areas of your life. Over the years I have seen so much misery caused by people's pursuit of one goal at the expense of all others. Let me give you some real-life examples.

I have a client, let's call her Sarah, who has built up a hugely successful business which is today worth at least £2 million. For more than 20 years, Sarah has worked at least 70 hours per week building her business and today she has all the trappings of success – a beautiful home, an exotic car and designer clothes. But the price she has paid for her success is her personal life. At 47, Sarah is single, childless and often lonely. With hindsight, she would have happily traded a large part of her success for a partner and family who love her.

I have another client, let's call him Bernie, who is of a similar age. Bernie is a wealthy man, but he has paid a heavy price for this success. Like Sarah, he worked more than 70 hours a week for many years. The relentless pressure, poor diet and lack of exercise caused him to have a heart attack at the age of 45. But it is not just his health that has suffered. Because of the hours he has worked, his wife and three children are virtual strangers to him. He recently told me how much he regrets missing his children grow up and how he fears that it is too late now to do much about it.

Both these people are rich, but are they successful? Neither of them has achieved much fulfilment from their success, and to my mind success without fulfilment is failure.

At the other extreme, one of my clients employs a manager, let's call him Paul, who seems to have the most wonderful family life. He has a wife he adores and four lovely children who worship him. Paul is home in time for dinner every night and spends every weekend pursuing hobbies with his children. But the price that he has paid is his career. At 54 years of age, Paul is in a job that he could do with his eyes shut and he has little prospect of further promotion. He confided to me during a management course how envious he is sometimes of his younger brother who has a high-flying job in the City.

Do you know someone like Sarah or Bernie or Paul – someone who has achieved success in one area of their lives by neglecting other areas? Take a moment to think about the consequences that this has had both for them and for the people they care about.

So many people get their work/life balance wrong. Unfortunately, by the time I get to meet them, it is often too late. That is the second prime objective of the Adam Walker Foundation: to encourage young people to set *balanced* goals for their lives right from the very outset.

Over the past 15 years, I have had the privilege of working with many thousands of people and, in my experience, happy people balance the goals that they want to achieve in many different areas. I am therefore going to suggest that you list the goals that you want to achieve in the future in no fewer than ten different categories. They are:

- financial goals

- career goals

- intellectual goals

- physical development

- emotional development

- close relationships

- living environment

- social life

- fun, hobbies and adventure

- contribution

Let's look at each of these areas in detail.

Financial goals

I'd like you to start by thinking of some specific goals that you would like to achieve in the financial area of your life. Even if money doesn't really motivate you, we all need a certain amount of money to live on – if you are constantly worrying about money, you will have less time to spend achieving the things that are more important to you.

- Start by writing down in your notebook some short-term financial goals, i.e. things that you would like to achieve within the next month.

- Then move on to some longer-term goals, i.e. things that you would like to achieve within the next year.

- Then move on to things that you would like to achieve within five years.

- Finally, think of things that you would like to achieve in the very long term, i.e. five years plus.

If you can't think what to write, just write the first thing that comes into your head. Trust your instincts – very often our subconscious mind knows more than we think. Don't worry at this stage about whether your goals are achievable. Don't worry either about getting things in the right category – for example, a goal such as saving the money to go on holiday might come under 'finance' or 'fun, hobbies and adventure'. Which category you put it into really doesn't matter.

The categories are just a way of making you think of as many things as possible.

The best way to do this exercise is to spend at least five minutes on each section. Try to keep the pen moving non-stop. This sort of automatic writing is a great way to draw out things from deep within your subconscious mind. Write down the goals that you would like to achieve financially now, before you read any further.

Now look at the list of goals you have put down and ask yourself another question: 'Are these goals ambitious enough?' It's a serious question. Most people find that a big goal has 100 times more power to motivate them than a modest one. The National Lottery is a great example of this. Most weeks the jackpot is around £5 million – enough to transform most people's lives. However, just occasionally there is a rollover jackpot that can reach £10 million or even £20 million. What happens to the ticket sales those weeks? They go through the roof. This is how human motivation works. So take a moment to review the goals that you have just put down and ask yourself again, 'Are these goals ambitious enough?' What would you put down if you knew that you couldn't fail? Well, write that down too!

Now go back through each of these goals again and put down a date by when you would like to achieve each of them. Don't agonise over each date. Just put down the first date that comes into your head. Trust your instincts. Take a couple of minutes and put those dates in now. Your first sheet should look something like this (see overleaf):

Financial goals

	Date for Achievement
Short-term goals (within next month) Pay John back the £100 I borrowed	31 January
Medium-term goals (within next year) Save money to go to Hawaii	31 December
Long-term goals (one to five years) Buy own house	April 2007
Very long-term goals (five years plus) Retire at 50 and travel the world	2035

Take a moment to read through your list one last time. Now I am going to ask you to think about those goals in a very specific way:

- Close your eyes and think about how you would feel if you had already achieved all of these things.

- Stand the way you would stand if you had already achieved all these financial goals.

- Breathe the way you would breathe if you had already achieved all of these things.

- See what you would see if you had already achieved all these things.

- Say what you would say to yourself if you had already achieved all these things.

- Feel the way you would feel if you had already achieved all these things.

By spending a few moments associating yourself with your goals in this way you will find that your motivation to achieve them will be increased exponentially. Take a few minutes to do this before you read on.

How did that feel? Pretty damn good, I should think. With that good feeling surging through your veins, move on quickly to the second category.

Career goals

The second area that I would like you to consider is your career. What sort of career do you want for yourself?

- Think of some specific career goals that you would like to achieve. Your next promotion perhaps, or possibly a complete career change? What would you put down here if you knew you could not fail? Put it down. The biggest goals are the ones that have the greatest power to motivate us.

- Take five minutes to write down everything that you can think of in this area. Again, some of your goals should be short-term goals, some medium-term, some longer-term. As before, try to keep the pen moving for at least five minutes and trust your instincts.

- Now, as before, go back through each of these goals and put down a date when you would like to achieve them by. Don't agonise over the decisions. Put down the first date that comes into your head. Trust your instincts. If necessary you can always change the dates later.

- Now take a few moments to review this list. How would you feel if you had already achieved all these things? How would you feel if you had already achieved everything that you wanted to achieve in your dream career?

Intellectual goals

The next area that I would like you to consider is your intellectual development. A lot of people think that their intellectual develop- ment finishes the day they leave school or college. They couldn't be more wrong. It is essential to keep stretching yourself intellec- tually throughout your life. If you don't, your brain will waste away like an unused muscle.

Many people find intellectual stimulation through their work. But if you are not working in an intellectually demanding job, there are many, many other ways to stretch your mind. Reading, writing, an engaging hobby, spending time with like-minded friends – whatever it is, the key is to do something that challenges your current beliefs and adds to the total of your knowledge.

Take some time to write down everything that you would like to achieve in this area – some books you would like to read perhaps, or a professional qualification that you would like to get. Again, try to think of things that you would like to achieve in the next month, the next year, the next five years and in the very long term.

Physical development

The next area I'd like you to set some goals for is your physical development. Many people neglect their health but, let's face it, unless you take care of your health and diet and find the time to exercise regularly, you won't be able to achieve any of the exciting things that you have put down in the other categories. At best you won't have the energy and at worst you'll be dead.

- Think of all the things that you would like to achieve in this area of your life and write them all down in your notebook. Think about your diet and your weight. Think about the amount of time you spend exercising. Think about your physical appearance.

- Write down a list of all the things that you would like to change in this area. As before, try to keep the pen moving for at least five minutes so that you access the desires that are buried deep within your subconscious mind.

Emotional development

My fifth category is emotional development. So many people I meet are handicapped by emotional issues, baggage from the past and feelings that are beyond their control. The extent of this unhappiness is quite breathtaking. I was horrified to read that 40 million people around the world take Prozac every day. In the UK alone 10 million people suffer from depression, a million people suffer with eating disorders such as anorexia or bulimia and millions more struggle with phobias, perfectionism or constant feelings of anger and guilt. And *tens* of millions are affected every day by unresolved issues from their childhood which cast a shadow over their adult lives.

Emotions such as fear, anger, guilt and love all have their place, but their role is to give depth and texture to our lives, not to control them. Do you control your emotions or do they control you?

Write down everything that you would like to change in this area of your life. For example:

- I would like to be able to control my temper better.

- I'd like to stop feeling angry whenever I think about my former husband/wife.

- I would like to feel less guilty about not making peace with my mother before she died.

If you have serious issues to address in this area, the specific goals that you write down may need to include a commitment to see a professional counsellor who is trained to help you to deal with the problem that is troubling you.

Close relationships

My next category is close relationships. This category would include the relationships that you have with your husband, wife or partner, your parents, your children, your brothers and sisters and other members of your immediate family.

Write down your goals in this area. What might they be?

- If you are already in a committed relationship, you might want to write down some things that you could do to improve it.

- If you are single, you might like to put down some things that you could do to find the ideal partner.

- If you have children, you might like to write down some things that you could to improve your relationship with them.

- If you don't yet have children and want them, why not write down how many children you would like to have, and when?

It's important when writing down your goals not to allow what you write to be tainted by compromise or, as some people might call it, 'realism'. Write down what you would really like to achieve. Write down the things that you would do if you knew you couldn't fail. All goals are inspiring, but big goals have a disproportionate capacity to inspire us.

Living environment

The home that we live in has such an important effect on our lives that I have given it a category all of its own.

Get a picture in your mind of your dream home.

- Is it a house or a flat?

- Is it a modern property or a period one?

- Is it in the country or in a town or city?

- How is it furnished?

Write down exactly what you would like to achieve in this area in the short term, the medium term and the long term.

Before we move on, take a moment to imagine how you would feel if you already lived in your dream home. How would it feel when you came home and saw it all lit up at night? How would it look bathed in sunshine on a beautiful spring morning or covered in frost on a cold winter's day?

Social life

Back to the present for category eight: your social life.

- What do you want to achieve in this area?

- Is there someone whom you have lost touch with but would like to see again?

- Would you like to know more people? If so, what could you do to achieve this?

- Write down everything that you would like to achieve or change in this category.

Fun, hobbies and adventure

You can really have some fun here!

- Write down all the fun things that you would like to do – bungee jumping, power boating, skiing, travelling to Outer Mongolia, seeing a real live whale, driving a Formula 1 racing car, learning to fly an aeroplane...

- Write down all the things you would like to do this month, this year and much later in life and then put some target dates in.

A surprising number of people find it difficult to write down their goals in this category because they feel that it is wrong to want things just for themselves. This is a very dangerous attitude. If you deny yourself such personal pleasures for too long, you will start to become resentful, and this resentment can all too easily start to affect your relationships with the people for whom you are sacrificing your pleasures – your family.

We all deserve some fun. Don't feel guilty about it. Don't wear a hair shirt all your life. No one will thank you for it. Just write down all the fun things you would like to do, the hobbies you would like to take up, the adventures you would like to have – and then make sure that you make time for them. (You can find out how in Chapter 6.)

Contribution

There is one final area that I would like you to set some goals for – an area that most people don't get round to thinking about until they have achieved a great deal of success in all the other areas. That area is spiritual and contribution goals. How could you give something back to others? What will be your legacy? What could you give that would make you feel really proud? It doesn't have to be money. Your contribution could be your time, your interest or something else that is of real value to others.

If my ten goal categories were to be arranged as a hierarchy, then contribution goals would be at the very top. The justification for this is demonstrated by the fact that so many of the world's most successful men and women take an interest in philanthropy later in their lives, once they have met all their needs in the other nine areas. They do so because they come to realise that helping others is where the greatest fulfilment can be found.

If you are going to get true fulfilment from your successes in all the other nine areas, you need to be able to ask yourself a question each week and come up with the right answer. That question is: 'What have I done to help others this week?'

- So, what could you contribute to others?

- Write down everything that you would like to achieve in this area in the short term, the medium term and the long term, and then put down some target dates.

Congratulations

Well, congratulations! You are now part of that tiny percentage of the population who have some written goals, and I cannot begin to tell you how these will change your life. I have done that exercise every year now for more than 20 years and I currently have 36 pages of things that I want to achieve and detailed plans about how I am going to achieve them. This list fills me with enthusiasm every time I read it.

I also have all my old journals with all my old goal lists going back over 20 years and I get a huge amount of satisfaction from rereading these from time to time. It's great fun to look at the goals I set for myself 5 or 10 or 20 years ago and realise how far I have come. Reading my goal lists gives me a deep sense of pride in what I have achieved so far, gratitude for what I already have and excitement about the things that I still have to look forward to. Above all, my goals give me a clear sense of purpose that allows me to greet each new day with genuine excitement and enthusiasm. Of course, I have made my share of mistakes along the way, but my sense of purpose has always served as a compass that has guided me through all the setbacks that have befallen me and helped me to make the right choices at the key times in my life.

Your top ten goals

Now you have your goal list, select the top ten goals that you want to focus on next year. Go back through all the goals that you have just written, pick the ten that are most important to you and list them in your notebook in order of importance.

You might also find it helpful to write them down on a larger piece of paper and stick it up somewhere where you can see it each day. This will serve as a constant reminder of things that are currently most important to you.

Your mission statement

The final thing you need is a mission statement – a statement that connects all these things together and gives you that sense of overall purpose for your own life. Let me give you mine:

> *The purpose of my life is to live with passion and integrity, to fulfil myself and to make a magnificent difference to the lives of others.*

This is my guiding principle and I test everything that I do against how well it helps me to meet this mission statement.

So what should your mission statement be? A personal mission statement comes from asking yourself fundamental questions such as:

- What do I want to achieve from my life?

- Why do I want to achieve this?

- What will it give me?

- What kind of person do I want to be?

- Why do I want to be that sort of person?

- What do I want to give?

- What is the purpose of my life?

- Why was I put here?

- What is my mission?

Excerpted from Franklin Covey's Sense of Purpose (To Leave a Legacy) *video, used with the permission of Franklin Covey. All rights reserved.*

FINDING YOUR MISSION STATEMENT

The next exercise will help you to find your mission statement. It's best to do it to the accompaniment of some quiet music if you can; I find that classical chamber music is best. You will also need your notebook and a pen, but this time I would suggest that you don't read the exercise in advance. Instead, put some music on, get your pen and paper ready, then read the questions overleaf and spend at least five minutes writing down everything that occurs to you in answer to those questions. Try to keep the pen moving in order to access your deepest thoughts. When you are sure you are ready, then turn the page...

- Life is short. So how will you live yours?
- What will make your life worth living?
- What is missing?
- How will you live?
- What will you learn?
- Who will you love?
- How will you show your love?
- How will you be remembered?
- What will be your legacy?
- What do you dream of?
- What is your fire within?
- What is your mission?

Write down everything that occurs to you in answer to these questions.

Excerpted from Franklin Covey's Sense of Purpose (To Leave a Legacy) *video. Used with the permission of Franklin Covey. All rights reserved.*

Well done; a lot of people find that quite an emotional exercise, but what I hope you will have gained from it is a clear idea of where you want to end up. What you probably have now is no more than a jumble of random thoughts, but I think that many of you will find that within these thoughts are the things that you really care about with such passion that they give you that burning sense of purpose.

So, from that jumble of thoughts you now need to distil a nice pithy sentence or two, a sentence that you can memorise, a sentence that ties all the things that you want to achieve together, a sentence that really inspires you. This will be your mission statement. This will be your passion. This will be what will inspire you to approach everything that you do with passion, vitality and enjoyment. This will be what will help you to achieve more, live more, love more, care more, be more and enjoy more than others around you.

- Take a few more minutes and try to come up with a sentence or two that capture the essence of everything that you have just written down. Don't try to make it perfect. You can always improve on it later. Just take up your notebook and write down the best sentence you can think of. Do it now.

I hope that you have been able to put down something, but don't worry if you haven't managed to do so. Sometimes a mission statement needs to be detected. It may come to you in a flash of inspiration in a few days' time. It may take a little longer. What I do know is that if you keep on asking the right questions then sooner or later you will come up with a mission statement that really inspires you.

The benefits of having a vision

In the second section of this book I am going to look at how you can set about the process of achieving some of your major goals, but before I do, let me tell you one last story about the benefits of having a vision. This story is not about a world leader or a successful businessman. It's about two bricklayers who lived 350 years ago.

A man was walking down a road and he came across a bricklayer. He asked the bricklayer what he was doing. 'I am laying bricks,' the man replied. 'I lay this brick on top of that one and then I am going to lay another brick on top of that. That is what I do – I am a bricklayer.'

The man walked on down the road, A few yards further on he came across a second bricklayer. The second bricklayer was smiling and whistling and was going about his work with the most enormous enthusiasm.

'What are you doing?' the man asked the second bricklayer.

'I am building St Paul's Cathedral,' the second bricklayer replied. 'It is going to be one of the finest buildings in the world and in 350 years' time it will be seen as a triumph of British architecture.'

Both men were, of course, doing the same job – but which one was enjoying his day's work more? The first had probably hauled himself out of bed that morning thinking, 'Oh dear, another boring day at work.' The second had leapt out of bed filled with excitement and enthusiasm for the day ahead of him. The only difference between them was that one had a clear sense of purpose.

PART TWO

Achieving your goals

CHAPTER 4

How to achieve a major goal

I told you earlier about how I wrote out my first goal list at the age of 22 and how within weeks, as if by magic, my dreams started to come true. At the time I really believed that some higher force was leading me towards my destiny. However, I have since discovered a much more scientific explanation. It's what psychologists call 'the reticular activating system'. The reticular activating system is the part of our brain that decides what we notice in a given situation. Let me give you an example of how it works.

A few months ago I was about to buy a new car, so I bought a magazine that listed all the cars that were available. In it there was an article about the Bristol Motor Company. The Bristol Motor Company makes only 200 cars a year and I don't think I had ever seen one on the roads before I bought that magazine. Nevertheless, the car looked wonderful in the photograph, so I sent off for a brochure. Do you know what? In the week that followed I saw no fewer than three Bristols driving around London! Coincidence, magic or the reticular activating system at work? I know what I think.

Every minute of every day our brains are bombarded by hundreds of stimuli, each of which is competing for our attention. During a typical day in London I see literally thousands of cars and these have to compete for my attention with literally tens of thousands of other things – advertising images, people passing by, traffic lights, road signs, the list is endless. My brain would go into meltdown if I tried to process all this information at once. The only way that it can cope is to absorb the information at a sub-conscious level – a sort of autopilot, if you like. The reticular activating system then constantly checks all the things that my brain has noticed subconsciously against the list of things that it knows that my conscious mind is interested in. When it makes a connection it sends a message to my conscious mind that enables me to say, 'Oh look, a Bristol! What a coincidence.'

I am sure that things like this happen to you on a regular basis. Perhaps you bought a new jacket on Saturday and saw a dozen other people wearing the same jacket on Monday morning. Perhaps you signed up for a charity parachute jump on Tuesday and suddenly found that every television show, radio programme and overheard conversation had a reference to parachuting. The reticular activating system is a very, very powerful force and all you have to do to enlist its help is to write your dreams down. That's why goal-setting is so powerful.

But there are some goals that won't be achieved quite as easily as this, so in this part of the book we are going to look at what you need to do to achieve your biggest, most important and most complex goals. When you have got something really big, complex and important to achieve it is essential to spend time planning exactly how you are going to achieve it. The process that I am going to share with you now is best explained with the aid of an example, so I am going to tell you about how I used it to achieve one of my major goals a few years ago.

I started with a goal. That goal was 100 per cent fitness. I wrote, 'I will be 100 per cent fit. I will be someone who is bursting with health, energy and vitality.'

The next thing that I did was to write down my current position in this area. I am ashamed to admit it, but at the time I was 63 lb (30 kg) overweight. Years of hotel lunches and insufficient exercise had taken their toll. But saying that I was unfit wasn't enough. I knew that in order to know what to focus on I would have to be far more specific. In order to do this I spent several hundred pounds on a whole battery of tests. I measured:

- my resting heart rate
- my heart rate after three minutes' exercise
- my flexibility and agility
- my percentage of body fat
- the precise fat content of my diet
- my cholesterol levels
- my blood pressure

The results really shocked me. I wasn't just out of shape, I was *very* out of shape, and I now had all the test results to prove it.

The next thing I did was to focus on why I had to make some changes in this area. Everything that I had ever read about psychology and human behaviour told me that unless I could come up with a strong enough reason to change my behaviour I would never be successful. Psychologists agree that all human behaviour is motivated by the desire to avoid pain or achieve pleasure. This principle serves us well most of the time. A child takes its first step and is rewarded with praise and a hug. So the child is encouraged to learn to walk. Later, the child touches a hot saucepan and is burned. So it learns not to touch hot things.

However, problems can arise if the pain or pleasure doesn't immediately follow the behaviour. Imagine a child who touched a hot saucepan in January and didn't get burned until April. That child would probably touch an awful lot of hot things during those three months. And when its hand started hurting in April it wouldn't necessarily associate the pain with the act of touching the hot saucepan three months previously.

This explains why we carry on doing so many of the things that we know are bad for us. Our subconscious minds are just not able to make the connection between the pleasure that we are feeling now and the pain that we might get in many years' time. If the moment you put a cream cake in your mouth your belly swelled up to twice its normal size, no one would ever overeat. If the very moment you lit a cigarette you could feel the searing pain of lung cancer, no one would smoke. But of course things don't happen this way. You can eat the cake at Christmas and not notice your trousers getting tight until the spring and you can smoke a cigarette at 20 and not feel the terrible pain of cancer until 30 or 40 years later. Fortunately, I knew enough about psychology to know how to make a connection between today's behaviour and tomorrow's pain. This is how I did it.

I wrote down all the worst consequences of continuing to be unfit. I thought of all the things that I had not been able to do because I wasn't fit enough. I thought about how unattractive I looked in my clothes. I thought of myself gasping for breath at the top of a single flight of stairs. Then I deliberately thought of some worse consequences still. I thought about how it would feel to have a heart attack at 40 and I actually imagined the pain that I might feel in my chest. I thought about the look on my wife's face as I took my last breath and I thought about the look on my children's faces as they said goodbye to their daddy at the graveside.

I carried on bombarding myself with the worst possible images. Then I imagined that instead of their happening to me in many years' time they were happening to me right now. I brought those images closer and closer in my mind. I made them bigger and bigger and brighter and brighter until it felt as if they were happening to me right then. I felt the terrible pain in my chest. I saw my wife's despair. I saw my children's tears. I saw all these things as if they were real. The whole process took only about half an hour, but by the time I had finished, I had a very different perspective on why I should make my health a much higher priority. Once you have a big enough reason why, the how becomes so much easier.

The next stage was to think of the specific strategies that would enable me to close the gap between where I was in this area and where I wanted to be. This was the easiest part. I knew exactly what I needed to do. The first strategy was to change my diet and the second was to exercise every day.

I knew, however, that thousands and thousands of people embark on a similar fitness plan every year and fail to keep it up, and I knew that I needed an extra step in my process. That extra step was to write down some measurable milestones, i.e. all the little tiny steps that I would take every day towards my outcome. I knew that these would be vital in maintaining my momentum and would give me the motivation to see the process through to completion. So under each of the strategies I wrote down dozens and dozens of tiny milestones. Under the exercise strategy I wrote:

- Milestone 1: Buy some running shoes. Date for achievement: 1 June.

- Milestone 2: Buy some exercise kit. Date for achievement: 2 June.

- Milestone 3: Buy a heart monitor. Date for achievement: 3 June.

- Milestone 4: Run as far as the garden gate. Date for achievement: 4 June.

- Milestone 5: Run as far as the big oak tree. Date for achievement: 5 June.

- Milestone 6: Run as far as the first stile. Date for achievement: 6 June.

- Milestone 7: Run as far as the second stile. Date for achievement: 7 June.

- Milestone 8: Run a quarter of a mile at 130 heartbeats per minute. Date for achievement: 13 June.

- Milestone 9: Run half a mile at 130 heartbeats per minute. Date for achievement: 20 June.

- Milestone 10: Run one mile at 130 heartbeats per minute. Date for achievement: 27 June.

- Milestone 11: Run two miles at 130 heartbeats per minute. Date for achievement: 14 July.

- Milestone 12: Run three miles at 130 heartbeats per minute. Date for achievement: 1 August.

- Milestone 13: Run four miles at 130 heartbeats per minute. Date for achievement: 14 August.

- Milestone 14: Run six miles at 130 heartbeats per minute. Date for achievement: 1 September.

I deliberately made the first few milestones very easy to achieve because I wanted to create a sense of momentum at the beginning of the process. Nevertheless, I took every single one of them very seriously. On 1 June I went to the local sports shop and bought some running shoes. In the same shop I was able to buy some exercise kit and a heart monitor. As soon as I left the shop I got my list out and solemnly ticked off the first three milestones. It was 1 June and I was already two days ahead of my schedule!

The following morning I got up early, put on my new running kit, strapped on my heart monitor and solemnly ran to the front gate. It was a ludicrously easy milestone – that's why I put it in! Nevertheless, as soon as I got back, I crossed that one off my list too. The next day I ran to the oak tree – a distance of about 200 yards. The next day I ran to the first stile. Each day I increased the distance just a little. After a week I was running a quarter of a mile. After two weeks I was running half a mile. After three weeks I was running a mile. Then two, then three, then four, then five. After eight weeks – two weeks ahead of my schedule – I was running six miles a day. I couldn't have run six yards when I started.

I continued to run every day for six months. As winter drew in, it got progressively harder, but whenever I felt like taking a day off I looked at all the milestones that I had ticked off and thought, 'It would be a terrible shame to stop now.'

The toughest test of all came six and a half months into my programme, on 23 December 1999. December is always a very busy time of year for me and I am often asked to speak at more than one conference in a day. Thursday 23 December was my last working day of the year and I had three separate speaking engagements to attend. I got up at 5 a.m. and drove to Warwickshire, where I had to present a business plan to around 100 people. Then I drove to Surrey to speak at a client's Annual General Meeting in the afternoon. Finally, I drove to central London, where I was due to speak at an evening awards ceremony. By the time I got home it was almost 1 a.m. I had made three speeches to a total of nearly 1,000 people. I had driven nearly 300 miles and I had been out of the house for nearly 19 hours. I was absolutely exhausted.

I entered my house through the back door so as not to wake the rest of my family. But as I crept through the back porch something really horrible caught my eye: my running shoes. 'Oh God,' I thought to myself, 'guess what I've been too busy to do today!'

I hesitated just for a moment. I looked outside. It was freezing cold and it had just started to drizzle. I cannot remember a time when a nice warm bed seemed more tempting. But I knew what I had to do. I knew that if I made an exception now it would be so much easier to make an exception next time. I remembered why I had set out on my fitness campaign and I called those terrible images of my children crying at their daddy's graveside back into my mind just for one fleeting moment. Then I put on my running gear and went out, into the darkness, the cold and the drizzle, to run my six miles.

The result of my fitness programme was that I lost 63 lb (30 kg) in six months and I can honestly say that I've never had a serious problem with my weight in all the years since then.

So how did I succeed in an area where so many other people fail? Well, the answer is that I followed a process and it's a process that will work just as well for you. Let me take you through it again in more detail so that you can apply it to achieving one of *your* major goals.

ACHIEVING A MAJOR GOAL

- I'd like you to start by thinking of your most important goal – a goal that really excites you. It's important to be specific. You need to phrase it in such a way that one day you will be able to say, 'Did I achieve it, yes or no?' For example, 'I will weigh 168 lb' is much better than 'I want to lose a bit of weight'.

- It is also important to make it an ambitious goal. Don't compromise or sell yourself short. What would you write down if you knew you couldn't fail? Well, why not write that down? Remember, big goals have a wholly disproportionate power to motivate us.

- Finally, make sure that you use really exciting language. 'I want to be recognised as the world's finest ballet dancer and be spoken of in the same breath as Margot Fonteyn' is so much more inspiring than 'I want to be a dancer'.

It's worth taking the time to get this right. It really is important to use language that is both precise and inspiring.

- Once you are absolutely happy both with your goal and with the language that you have used to express it, write it down on a fresh page in your notebook.

- Next, write down your current position in this area. Again, try to be as precise as possible. Remember how I spent money on a whole batch of medical tests to be sure that I knew exactly what stage of health and fitness I was in.

- The next step is to write down why you must succeed in this area. What would success in this area give you? What would it give the people you care about? What would failure in this area cost you? What would it cost those you care about? Be sure to think about the effects of failure on the people you love. Often we will do far more for others than we will do for ourselves. It is very important to make these images as dramatic as possible. I found the thought of dying prematurely of a heart attack to be pretty distressing, but the image that was even more powerful was the image of my wife and children grieving at my graveside.

Once you are sure that you have put down every single consequence of success and failure, you need to take the time actually to go to those places in your mind. To do this properly you will need a quiet room where you will be undisturbed for at least 20 to 30 minutes. Some people find that classical music played quietly helps their concentration.

Sit yourself down comfortably and ask yourself these questions:

- Why do I want to achieve this goal?

- What would success in this area give me?

- What would success in this area give the people I care about?

- How would I feel if I had already achieved this goal?

Now close your eyes and take a few moments to conjure up images in your mind of yourself having already achieved this goal.

Next ask yourself:

- What would failure in this area cost me?

Take time to think of all the worst consequences and bring these images into your mind.

Then ask yourself:

- What would failure in this areas cost those I care about?

Think of the most horrible consequences of failure and bring these images into your mind. Now think of some worse images still!

Now in order to get the maximum power from this exercise you will need to read through the five bullet points below several times until you have memorised them. Then close your eyes and work through each in turn. Allow yourself several minutes to reflect on all the images that you conjure up.

- Bring the images closer and make them bigger and bigger and brighter and brighter.

- Make sure that they are in full colour.

- Now turn them into a moving picture.

- Now put yourself into the movie.

- Now imagine that all these terrible things are actually happening to you right now, right this very second.

If you did that exercise properly, it will have been quite an emotional experience, but it will also have been a very worthwhile one. How do you feel about achieving your goal now? Will you give up at the very first hurdle or will you do whatever it takes to achieve your outcome?

Once you have found a big enough reason to succeed, the next stage in the process is to think about how you are going to go about achieving your goal. Motivation alone will not be enough to achieve your outcome. You also need a plan. So you will need to spend some time thinking about the strategies that are most likely to enable you to achieve your outcome.

Experience tells me that the best way to do this is to start with a scatter list of as many possibilities as you can come up with, so write down lots of ways of achieving your goal. Don't worry about whether they are good ideas or bad ideas. Just write down as many different ways as you can think of. Once you are sure you have thought of as many as you can, pick out the most workable ones and write them down.

The final step in turning your dream into a reality is to break down each of these strategies into tiny milestones, i.e. the things that you will need to do on a daily basis to make progress towards achieving your goal. Each milestone needs to have a date by which you will achieve it and you will need a column in which you can tick each one off once you have done it. Be very careful not to be too optimistic with your target dates. If you start missing them, it is all too easy to become demoralised and give up on your goal altogether. If in doubt, put a later date in. These milestones will pay an absolutely crucial role in making your dream come true. Without them it is so very easy to get overwhelmed by the sheer enormity of a task or discouraged by your apparent lack of progress in the early days.

The finished document should be so precise that someone who had never met you would be able to follow the process and achieve the same result.

To summarise, the process is:

Step 1. State goal.

Step 2. State current position.

Step 3. Write down why you must succeed.

Step 4. List strategies: '*How* will I do it?'

Step 5. Break down each strategy into detailed milestones: 'How will I *measure* my progress?'

This simple five-step process will play a hugely important role in helping you to make any dream become a reality.

CHAPTER 5

How to harness the power of your subconscious mind

The ideas that I have shared with you so far are techniques that are designed to appeal primarily to the conscious mind. But remember that the subconscious mind is considered to be approximately 30,000 times more powerful than the conscious mind. So if you are going to give yourself the very best chance of achieving your goals, you are going to need to know how to harness the power of your subconscious.

A great way to understand the connection between the two is to imagine a huge Roman galleon powered by 30,000 slaves shackled together in rows. A ferocious slave master ensures that the oarsmen work ceaselessly day and night powering the boat forwards as fast as it can go. The conscious mind, in this metaphor, would be the helmsman, who with just a flick of his wrist has the power to decide whether the power of 30,000 oarsmen is used to power the boat forwards, backwards or round and round in circles. This is precisely how your subconscious mind works: it toils tirelessly 24 hours a day trying to give you the things that you want. But it cannot decide which direction to travel in – that's your job. If you are going to achieve all your dreams, you simply must learn how to communicate with your subconscious mind. So how can you do this?

By far the best way to communicate with your subconscious

mind is through pictures. Take a moment to think about the logic of this. The only glimpse that most of us get into our subconscious minds is when we dream at night. And how do we dream? In pictures. I have read literally hundreds of books on personal development during the last 20 years, and time after time they talk about the benefits of having 'a clear picture in your mind of exactly what you want to achieve'. More recent books have a special term for this technique: they call it 'visualisation'.

The power of visualisation

Before we go on, let me give you a very powerful demonstration of the power of visualisation.

- Stand up and find a space where you are at least an arm's length away from the wall or any other obstruction.

- Stand with your feet together facing forwards and your arms hanging loosely by your sides.

- Lift your right arm up until it is horizontal, at 90 degrees to your body, and point at something that is directly in front of you.

- Now, keeping your feet pointing straight ahead, turn clockwise, moving your arm round until it has gone as far as it can without straining. Note the point in the room that your arm is now pointing at.

- Now turn back towards the front.

You will need to read through the next part of this exercise in its entirety before attempting it.

- Close your eyes and imagine that you are turning your arm round again until you reach the same point that you reached last time. Don't do it, just imagine it in your mind.

- Now imagine yourself turning your arm past the point that you just reached and in one easy fluid movement turning it much, much further than you did before.

- Rehearse the movement five or six times in your mind. Imagine your arm swinging easily and effortlessly past the point you reached last time and then going on much, much further than it did last time.

- Then open your eyes and turn your arm as far as you can.

Ninety-five per cent of people find that they are able to turn their arm further the second time than they did the first. Such is the power of visualisation.

So how is this possible? The answer is that the subconscious mind cannot distinguish between the things that it has actually done and the things that it has imagined that it has done. And because your subconscious mind thinks that you have turned your arm this far once, it helps you to do so again.

Now just imagine what would happen if you were able to apply the power of visualisation to all your other goals. Just think how much easier they would be to achieve. Well, I have some great news for you: you can. The power of visualisation can be applied to anything that you want to achieve. If you visualise your goals, if you create pictures in your mind of exactly what you want to achieve, you will be amazed at how quickly your subconscious mind starts to find new ways to help you to achieve them.

There are countless examples of famous people applying this principle to get what they wanted. Jack Nicklaus, the golfer, said that golf is 90 per cent preparation and only 10 per cent skill'. He visualises each putt before he makes it. Michael Johnson, Olympic gold-medal winner and world-record holder, said that he actually saw himself running with perfect form – and winning the race – before it had even begun. Gymnast Mary Lou Retton said that the night before she competed in the Olympics she lay in bed and mentally rehearsed her performance. She imagined herself going through the routine. She saw her body performing the moves; she felt the impact as her hands grabbed the bars. She imagined herself performing all her routines perfectly, seeing herself going through all the moves with charm, poise and confidence. The result was a perfect performance – and a gold medal.

What worked for them will work for you, too. So before you read on, take a moment to visualise yourself having already achieved your most important goal.

- If your goal is to be a doctor, for example, visualise a perfect moment in your surgery – a moment that encapsulates everything that makes you want to become a doctor. Don't skimp on the detail. Think about how you would like your desk to look and how you would like your consulting room to be furnished. Get a clear picture of a patient. What do they look like? What ailment are you treating them for? What are they saying to you? How are they expressing their gratitude for all the help that you have given them? How does this gratitude make you feel?

- If your goal is to become fit, visualise a perfect moment that encapsulates what fitness means for you – hitting the winning shot in a game of tennis, perhaps, or trying on some beautiful new clothes. Get a picture clearly in your mind of yourself enjoying that perfect moment, then add layer upon layer of detail. What time of year is it? What is the weather like? What are you wearing? Who are you sharing your perfect moment with? The more detailed you make the picture, the more powerful the effect on your motivation will be.

I bet that felt good, didn't it? But while visualisation is a powerful and well-proven way to make your dreams come true, it has its limitations. Perhaps its greatest limitation is that you cannot keep it up for very long. No matter how hard you try and no matter how desperately you want to achieve your goal, you will find your attention will begin to wander after just a few minutes. As soon as other images start to enter your head, the power of visualisation is diluted. Fortunately there is a solution to this problem, and it's a solution that is so simple that I can summarise it in three words:

Draw some pictures.

It really is as simple as that. In order to harness the magical power of visualisation 24 hours a day, all you need to do is to draw some pictures. However, in order to get the very maximum impact you will need to use a very specific type of picture in a very specific way. Some people try to use pictures that they have cut out from magazines and newspapers. These simply will not do. We are bombarded with images like this every day through television, advertising and the media. In order to make your images really different and really special, they *must* be images that you have drawn yourself. Now I expect that some of you are thinking, 'But I can't draw.' Well, don't worry, that really doesn't matter. The quality of the drawing is completely irrelevant. All that matters is what the drawing symbolises to you. If you can draw a stick man then you can draw well enough to complete this exercise.

DRAWING YOUR GOALS

Here's how to go about it:

- Choose your biggest, most complex and most important goal – the one that you would give almost anything to achieve.

- Now draw a picture of yourself having achieved it. The picture need only be symbolic, but it must also encapsulate all the joy, pride and satisfaction that you will feel when you have accomplished your goal. For example, if your goal is to lose some weight, draw a picture of yourself as you would like to look, trying on a fabulous new outfit. Draw this picture at the top of a fresh page in your notebook, as shown in the diagram overleaf.

- Now underneath this picture write in the date by which you want to achieve this goal.

- Once you have done this, at the bottom of the page draw a picture that symbolises your current position and put today's date in underneath it.

- Now think about how you will go about closing the gap between where you are now and where you want to be. What strategies will

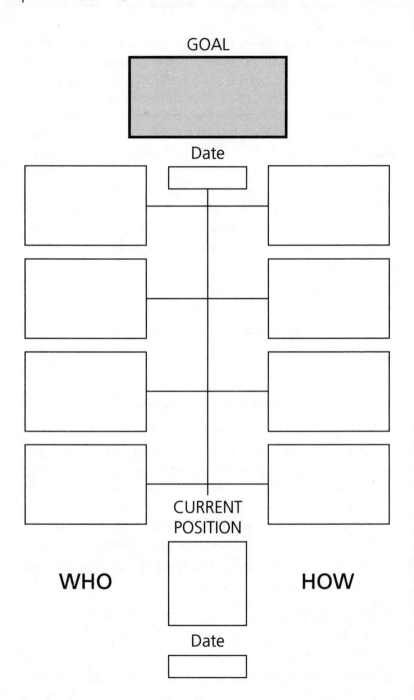

you employ to achieve your goal? Pick three or four of the most important ones and draw some pictures on the right-hand side of the page that symbolise these actions. For example, to lose weight one of your strategies might be to exercise regularly, so you could draw a picture of yourself at an exercise class.

- Next think about some of the people who might be able to help you to achieve your goal and draw some pictures of them in the boxes on the left-hand side of the page. For example, you might draw a picture of your aerobics instructor.

- Finally, take some time to colour each of the pictures in. Most of us dream in colour and your images will be far more powerful if they are in Technicolor.

- When you have finished your drawing, hang it up next to your bed. Ideally, it should be in a place where you can see it when you are lying down with your head on your pillow.

- Before you go to sleep each night, take 30 seconds to look at your picture. By doing this you will direct your subconscious mind to spend the whole night dreaming up ways to help you to achieve your goal.

Of all the techniques that I teach at my seminars this is probably the most powerful and I have been told many extraordinary stories about the results that people have achieved with it.

One of the most powerful stories of all, and one that I can tell you without betraying any confidences, is a story about my wife Kym, who completed a goal picture in May 2001. Kym is a writer. She has written all her life and she had already achieved some measure of success. However, with our children growing up and needing less of her time, she wanted to take her writing to the next level and to be taken seriously as a novelist. With this outcome in mind, she sat down to prepare her goal picture.

The first principle that Kym applied was the principle that big goals have a disproportionate capacity to inspire us. She asked herself questions like:

- What do I really want to achieve?
- What would I put down if I could have my life any way that I wanted it to be?
- What would I put down if I knew that I couldn't fail?

Great questions produce great answers. Kym wrote down:

I want to win the Man Booker Prize for literature.

Is this is a big goal? It most certainly is. The Man Booker Prize is one of the most prestigious literary prizes in the world. Does it have the power to motivate Kym? You bet – she'd go to hell and back to achieve this.

At the top of her sheet Kym drew a picture of herself on stage receiving the Man Booker Prize and put in her target date of November 2005. It's a lovely picture that completely encapsulates the joy that she would feel at winning such a prestigious award.

Next Kym drew a picture that symbolised herself in her current situation as a writer of short stories, poetry and magazine articles, and put in the then current date of May 2001. On the right-hand side she drew six pictures that symbolised some of the key things that she would need to do to win the Man Booker Prize, for example finishing the first draft of her novel, finishing the second draft, finding an agent and finding a publisher – no small feats in a difficult publishing climate.

On the left-hand side Kym drew pictures of some of the people from whom she would need help along the way. She drew a picture of her writing mentor and a symbolic picture of the agent who she hoped would represent her. She drew a lady with short black curly hair wearing an orange jumper. Her finished drawing is shown on pages 60–61.

Kym hung her drawing on the arm of her bedside light and looked at it for a few moments before she went to sleep each night. Each day she worked hard to complete the first, second and final drafts of her novel. More than a year later, in July 2002, she finally finished it. She sent the manuscript to one of the most prestigious literary agents in the country, Curtis Brown. To her delight they responded almost by return of post and said that they would like to meet her. The meeting was arranged for two weeks later, on Thursday 4 July.

Kym knew that this was an opportunity that most writers would give anything for and she could hardly bear to wait for the meeting. Finally, the day arrived. Because it was such an important meeting, Kym arrived in plenty of time and waited nervously in the reception area. At 10 a.m. precisely the receptionist showed her into her prospective agent's office. She was an attractive woman in her early fifties *with short black curly hair*, wearing black trousers and *an orange jumper*. Kym took one look at her and just knew that everything was going to be all right. Her nervousness left her in seconds. She was able to give an excellent account of herself during the meeting and an hour later she had agreed terms with Curtis Brown to represent her.

Some people might think that this was no more than a remarkable coincidence. After all, lots of people have curly black hair and lots of people wear orange jumpers. Well, perhaps the story so far could be a coincidence, but it doesn't end there. On the way home Kym read through some of the literature that Curtis Brown had given her. She was delighted to find that her new agent also represented Margaret Atwood, the previous year's winner of the Booker Prize! Even this could still be a coincidence. But the story doesn't end here either.

Six weeks later I told this story for the very first time to a group of 100 girls at St Helens School in Northwood. I was giving a seminar on goal-setting and this story seemed a wonderful example of how the process had worked for someone else. I had never told this story in public before. At precisely the same moment that I was telling her story Kym received a telephone call from her agent. She wanted to let Kym know that she had just clinched a deal with Hodder and Stoughton to publish her novel *Erskine's Box*. She had managed to secure great terms – a two-book deal, a very substantial advance and lead-title status.

The story does not end there. Hodder and Stoughton were so

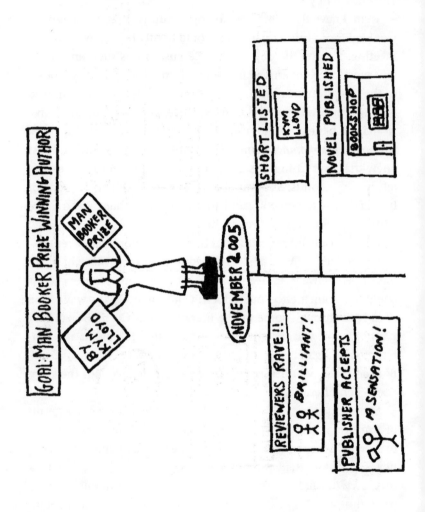

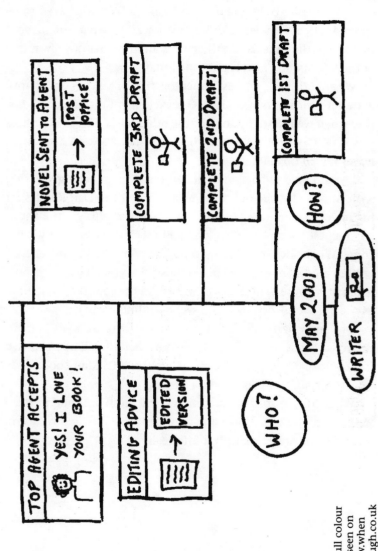

Kym's original full colour
drawing can be seen on
our website www.when
successisnotenough.co.uk

impressed by Kym's first novel that they chose it as their entry for the Author's Club Best First Novel Award 2003. Each publisher is allowed to enter only one title, so Kym felt honoured even to be entered. Their confidence in her was rewarded when she made it through to the shortlist. In the judges' opinion her novel was one of the best six first novels published that year.

We attended the awards dinner together in Mayfair on 22 April with our hearts in our mouths. Our excitement increased still further when we found that one of the other five shortlisted authors was D. B. C. Pierre, who won the 2003 Man Booker Prize for his novel *Vernon God Little*.

I would love to be able to finish this story by telling you that Kym won. Sadly, she did not. The award went to Dan Rhodes for his novel *Timoleon Vieta Come Home* (he was also on the list of Granta Best Young Novelists 2003). But look just how far Kym has come. When she sat down to do that drawing she had never even written a full-length novel before. Just four years later she is on a shortlist with some of the finest writers in the country. Sometimes even I am astonished by the power of setting goals.

Oh, and one last thing. At the time of writing Kym has just delivered her second novel, *The Book of Guilt*. It will be published in November 2004 – just in time to win the 2005 Man Booker? My fingers remain firmly crossed for her.

While this inspirational story is still fresh in your mind, I would urge you to sit down and draw a picture of your own dream and how you are going turn it into reality.

CHAPTER 6

How to find more time

'I meant to do it, but I've been so busy.'

Have you ever said that? It is by far the most common excuse that I hear when I ask people why they haven't made more progress towards achieving their goals. The way that people plan and use their time is, in my experience, the single most important factor in determining whether they achieve their goals or just talk about them.

My objective in this chapter is not to give you yet another fancy time-management system – there are plenty of those around already. My aim is to show you how to make enough time in a busy schedule to make progress towards achieving your goals, and to show you a system that will help you to maintain a proper balance in your life, however busy you are.

So much to do...

The system that most people use to manage their time is, in my opinion, outdated, demoralising and extremely inefficient. Let me show you what I mean.

- Open your notebook at a fresh page and from memory write a list of everything that you have to do tomorrow. It is important to make sure that this list includes everything. Not just the big things, but details like collecting your suit from the dry cleaner's and booking the car in for its service.

- Read through the list that you have just written. How does reading that list make you feel – energised and excited about the coming day or stressed and overwhelmed?

- Now take a moment to plan how you might fit all those things into your day.

- Now ask yourself another question: what chance is there that your day will actually work out like this? Do you think that you will be able to work peacefully through your list dealing with each item in order of priority or will it be another day when interruptions and unforeseen emergencies get in your way? And if you don't manage to finish your list, how will that make you feel? How will you feel at the end of the day when you look at your 'to do' list and see that 92 things still remain on it – even more stressed, I expect?

Perhaps the worst thing of all about 'to do' lists is that even on those rare days when we do manage to tick everything off, there's no reward. Finishing your list makes you feel good for about 30 seconds. But then you remember that tomorrow you will just have to face another long list of things to do. Let me recommend a better system to you.

The principles of effective time management

The first essential of effective time management is to plan a week at a time, not just a day. Only by planning a whole week at a time can you ensure that there is a proper balance between your work time and your home time. I find that Sunday evening is the best time to sit down and think about the week ahead, but you can choose whatever time suits you.

The second principle is to treat the time that you need to spend working towards your goals as your number-one priority. This means putting it in the diary first. This is the only way to ensure that it doesn't get crowded out of the busy schedule by other (less important) demands.

The third principle is to make sure that you find time in every week for leisure activities and plan these with the same care with which you plan your work life. Maintaining the right balance between home and work is the key to long-term success and fulfilment. In Chapter 3 I suggested maintaining this balance by dividing your goals into ten categories (financial, career, close relationships, etc.). This works well for a goal-setting exercise. However, these may be too many categories to include in your diary on a day-to-day basis. I now therefore recommend that people think about their day-to-day lives in terms of the different *roles* that they play.

These roles should be chosen to reflect your current priorities, i.e. the areas of your life in which you want to make improvements. Currently mine are:

1. Husband

2. Father

3. Businessman

4. Author

5. Charity trustee

6. Investor

7. Individual

Everyone's roles are different. Here are some more real-life examples:

John –

1. Salesman
2. Office manager
3. Future area manager
4. Son
5. Casanova!
6. Amateur racing driver
7. Individual

Theresa –

1. Wife
2. Mother
3. Homemaker
4. School governor
5. Magistrate
6. Daughter
7. Individual

Yolanda –

1. Medical student
2. Future doctor
3. Daughter
4. Hockey player
5. Head of the student union
6. Political activist
7. Individual

YOUR ROLES AND GOALS

● Before you read on, take a few moments to write down the main roles that you need to play in your life at the moment. Most people find that six plus themselves as an individual is about the right number to focus on, but there is no magic about having six – you can have a few more or a few less, whatever suits you.

- Start by writing down your chosen roles in your notebook, running across the top of the page (*see the charts on pages 74 –77*). Now turn back to your goal list and pick out the goals that you want to make some progress with during the coming week. Now decide which role each goal comes under and write each one beneath the appropriate role heading.

- Before you go any further, take a moment to look at each goal in turn and ask yourself these questions:

1. What is my final goal in this area?
2. Why *must* I achieve this goal?
3. What will achieving this goal give me?
4. What would failing to achieve this goal cost me?
5. What would failing to achieve this goal cost the people I care about?
6. What actions can I take next week to make progress towards achieving this goal?

- You need to do this for *each goal in turn*. It might seem a little long-winded at first, but believe me, unless you constantly remind yourself why each goal is important to you, your motivation to achieve it will fade and you will start to allow other things to get in the way. Ask yourself:

  – What do I want to achieve?

  – Why *must* I achieve it?

  – How can I make progress in this area next week?

These are the three key questions that will maintain your commitment and so ensure that whatever else you don't have time to do next week, you will find the time to make progress towards achieving your goals.

- In this state of determination and commitment, write down the milestones that you want to achieve in the appropriate place under each goal.

A finished goal might look like this:

- Ultimate outcome: to double the turnover of my business.

- Why *must* I achieve it? To fulfil my potential, achieve my destiny and give my family the standard of living that they deserve.

- What would it cost me if I failed to achieve this goal? My self-respect and credibility.

- What would failure cost the people I care about? My children might not be able to go to college. This could prevent them from fulfilling their potential.

- How can I make progress next week in this area? Design a new website.

- What are the milestones I could achieve in this area? Write copy, meet designer and meet e-marketing people.

You need to work through this system in this amount of detail for each of your goals.

Once you have finished, take a few moments to make sure that you have made time to care for yourself as an individual. If you don't, you will be like a car that is never serviced. You will start to go more and more slowly until one day you will break down altogether. It is essential to find time in every week to care for yourself in four key areas. These are:

- *Your body.* Have you made time during the week to exercise and care for yourself physically?

- *Your mind.* You need to diarise time to read or to find some other way to stretch yourself intellectually.

- *Your heart.* You need to diarise time to spend with the people you love or pursuing the hobbies that give you pleasure.

- *Your soul.* Diarise time to give something back, for example through charity work, religious worship or just perhaps helping a friend.

The Red Cross is the world's largest
independent humanitarian movement,
and often the only organisation able
to cross borders to bring help
wherever it is needed.

Please use this bookmark to let
others know about the work of the
British Red Cross, inspiring them
perhaps to support us as you do.

Get life-saving skills at your fingertips
with the free British Red Cross
first aid app. Download it now at:
redcross.org.uk/app

Supporting the

 British Red Cross

The British Red Cross Society,
incorporated by Royal Charter 1908, is a
charity registered in England and Wales
(220949) and Scotland (SC037738).

44 Moorfields
London EC2Y 9AL
0844 87 100 87
redcross.org.uk

RB

Season's
Greetings

The whole process might take as much as an hour. However, I promise you that if you do it properly you will more than make up this hour during the week, because it will transform your levels of motivation, productivity and effectiveness.

- When you have finished, take a few moments to review your new 'to do' list.

- Now how do you feel when you look at this list – stressed and overwhelmed, or excited and passionate about all the wonderful things that you have to look forward to in the week ahead?

Many of the items on the new list will of course be the same items that were on the last one. So what has changed? What has changed is that even the most mundane activities are now connected to your ultimate purpose.

Now schedule it

Planning your diary a week at a time and connecting each item to your goals will transform your levels of motivation and productivity. However, in order to ensure that these things actually get done, you will need to do one last thing: schedule them.

The importance of this was brought home to me a few years ago when I attended a business-plan review meeting with one of my clients. Twelve branch managers were present. The purpose of the meeting was to review their actual performance against the business plans I had helped them to create 12 months previously. I knew in advance of the meeting that three managers had missed their target, eight had achieved it and one had shattered it.

We dealt with the three managers who had failed to meet their targets first. In every case, either they had failed to put their milestones into their diaries at all or they had written them in and then allowed them to be squeezed out by more urgent but less important matters.

The eight managers who had achieved their targets had all taken their milestones much more seriously. They had obviously all taken the time to read their business plans on a regular basis and had put their milestones into the diary well in advance. By and large, they had done most of what they said they were going to do at the times when they had said they were going to do it.

The last manager had achieved a magnificent result. Despite starting the year as already the top office in the group, he had achieved an astonishing 65 per cent increase in turnover over the previous year. I asked him how he had scheduled his milestones.

'Well,' he said, 'the day after my business plan was signed off I shut myself in the back office with the business plan, the office diary, everyone's individual diaries and the year's holiday rota and I scheduled in every single milestone for the entire year ahead. Once they were in the diary they were set in stone. I made it clear to everyone that achieving our milestones was to be given priority over everything else and that nothing short of an earthquake would be accepted as an excuse for failing to complete a milestone on the agreed date.'

I have never met anyone with quite such a focused approach. An extreme example perhaps, but his results spoke for themselves. I think that everyone in that room will remember the lesson that they learned from him that day.

SCHEDULE YOUR MILESTONES

- While this story is still fresh in your mind, look back in your notebook to your own milestones.

- Now start allocating them to an appropriate spot in next week's diary.

- Start by putting in the fixed meetings – things that have to be done at a particular time and cannot be moved.

- Then put in time to work on your major goals and milestones. Make an estimate of how long each one will take and try, if possible, to allocate it to a specific time slot.

- When doing so, be sure to take account of your personal biorhythms. Some of us are morning people, some of us are night owls. If something is important it should be scheduled for whatever time of day you feel at your very best.

- Make sure you include your leisure activities in your plan. If you don't, it's all too easy to find that work encroaches on your leisure time and your life starts to get out of balance.

- Minor jobs like booking the car in for a service should be written in the 'other tasks' section and allocated to a day but not a specific time. They can be filled in around the bigger tasks on the day itself.

- Finally, don't be too ambitious about what you can achieve each day. Interruptions are almost inevitable and it's best to recognise this by scheduling in some extra unstructured time.

- At the start of each day take a moment to check your rough plan, then incorporate it into whatever time-management system you use to plan your time on a daily basis.

REVIEWING YOUR PROGRESS

At the end of each week, take a few moments to review the previous week's plan and ask yourself three questions:

- What were my greatest achievements this week?

- What were my greatest disappointments?

- What lessons can I learn for the future?

If you have any remaining doubt about the value of this system, try it for a couple of weeks and then decide. In my experience you will almost certainly find that the results that you achieve will persuade you to use it for ever more.

Dealing with interruptions

The very first principle that is taught on most time-management courses is the principle of creating 'priority time', i.e. time that is free from interruptions. This is fundamental. You will never get anything done if you allow yourself to be constantly at everyone else's beck and call. But however carefully you plan your day, some interruptions are inevitable. So how should you go about dealing with them?

My first recommendation is that you allow a certain amount of time for interruptions and schedule this 'unstructured time' into your diary. This won't reduce the number of interruptions that you have to put up with, but it will certainly do a great deal to reduce your stress levels!

If someone or something does interrupt you, you need to take an informed decision as to whether to continue doing what you had planned to do or to allow the interruption to disrupt your schedule. A great way to make this decision is to weigh up each choice in terms of both its urgency and its importance. Most activities will come into one of four categories:

1. *Not urgent and not important*, for example lying on the sofa flicking aimlessly between TV channels. This is the lowest-grade activity of all. When you are busy doing this, an interruption will probably be welcome.

2. *Urgent but not important*, for example when a salesman wants to talk to you about a product that you don't want to buy. He is demanding your immediate attention, but the conversation is not important to you. It's so very easy to fritter your time away on activities like this.

3. *Urgent and important*, for example meeting a deadline for a crucial newspaper advertisement that is due in one hour's time. A certain percentage of tasks will always fall into this category. However, if the task was that important perhaps you should have planned to start it a little sooner.

4. *Important but not urgent,* for example spending an hour exercising. There is no urgency about this and it's so easy to allow it to be crowded out of a busy schedule. But if you put it off for too long the day will come when your body will let you down and prevent you from doing any of the other things that you want to do.

Your objective should be to spend as much of your time as possible on category-four activities.

If you decide that the interruption is unavoidable, ask yourself three questions:

1. What would happen if I didn't do this?

2. Do I really have to do it myself?

3. Does it have to be done now?

If you still feel that you need to allow the interruption, be sure to take a moment before you break off to diarise a revised time to complete your original task.

The strategies that I have outlined in this chapter won't, of course, give you more time. However, they will allow you to spend more of your time on the things that matter most to you, and that is what this book is about.

Roles	Husband	Father	Business	Author	Charity trustee	Investor	Individual
Goal 1	Organise anniversary	Teach H to play chess	New website	Finish book	Appoint PR company	Sell shares in X	**Body**
Milestone 1	Book restaurant	Buy board	Shortlist designers	500 words per day for 4 days	Agree budget	Check on CGT liability	Run 3 times
Milestone 2	Order flowers	Buy rule book	Shortlist marketing companies		Research shortlist	Call broker	Yoga 3 times
Milestone 3	Buy present	Play first game	1st draft copy		Arrange 3 pitches		Karate twice
Milestone 4	Buy card						Chiropodist
Goal 2		Research next school	Venue for AGM			Buy shares in Y	**Mind**
Milestone 1		Obtain league tables	Ring X for recommendation			Study chart	Finish book
Milestone 2		Compile shortlist	Agree budget			Read annual report	Watch TV documentary
Milestone 3		Get dates of open days	Finalise numbers			Decide on stop loss policy	
Milestone 4			Compile shortlist for John			Place order with broker	
Goal 3		Teach I new guitar piece					**Heart**
Milestone 1		Buy music					Meal out with K

chart continues

Roles	Husband	Father	Business	Author	Charity trustee	Investor	Individual
Milestone 2		Buy CD					
Milestone 3							
Milestone 4							
Goal 4							**Soul**
Milestone 1							Help at Scout jumble sale
Milestone 2							
Milestone 3							
Milestone 4							

Other Tasks

	Husband	Father	Business	Author	Charity trustee	Investor	Individual
	MOT K's car	Mend I's puncture	Dinner jacket to cleaners	Get sales report for last book			Research new boat engine
							Mend light in woodshed

NEXT WEEK'S PRIORITIES FORM

Roles	Role 1	Role 2	Role 3	Role 4	Role 5	Role 6	Role 7
Goal 1							Body
Milestone 1							
Milestone 2							
Milestone 3							
Milestone 4							
Goal 2							Mind
Milestone 1							
Milestone 2							
Milestone 3							
Milestone 4							
Goal 3							Heart
Milestone 1							
Milestone 2							
Milestone 3							
Milestone 4							

chart continues

Roles	Role 1	Role 2	Role 3	Role 4	Role 5	Role 6	Role 7
Goal 4							Soul
Milestone 1							
Milestone 2							
Milestone 3							
Milestone 4							
Other Tasks							

PART THREE

Overcoming obstacles

CHAPTER 7

Obstacles are inevitable

Y ou have got a great plan. However, it is very unlikely that it will be as easy to achieve in practice as it looks on paper. Obstacles and setbacks are inevitable and, if you are serious about turning your dreams into reality, it is essential that you spend some time now thinking about how you are going to overcome them.

WHAT ARE YOUR OBSTACLES?

A great way to predict the obstacles that you are most likely to encounter is to look back at last year. Take a few moments to answer these questions:

- What was your greatest disappointment last year?

- What other setbacks did you encounter last year?

- Which of last year's goals did you fail to achieve?

- What were the main obstacles to success last year?

It's reasonable to assume that you will encounter many of the same obstacles again next year.

With last year's setbacks clearly in your mind, take your notebook and write a list of the things that might stop you from achieving next year's goals.

I am going to show you how to deal with all the obstacles you have written down, but before I do so, let me tell you a story about someone who had to deal with far more obstacles than most of us. His name was Art Berg and he spoke at a conference that I attended in Florida in January 2000. His 45-minute speech was one of the most powerful and moving presentations that I have ever heard.

Art Berg told us what happened to him on Christmas Day 1983. When he woke up that morning everything in his life was perfect. He was 21 years old, in outstanding physical shape and due to marry his childhood sweetheart in five weeks' time. Art believed that God had great plans for his future. But they were not to be.

At 7 o'clock in the evening Art set off with a friend on the 15-hour drive to Utah so that he could spend the rest of the holiday with his fiancée. Art drove the first half of the journey, then let his friend take the wheel. About an hour later he was woken up with a jolt. His friend had fallen asleep at the wheel. The car hit the cement barriers and rolled over several times. His friend walked away from the accident with no more than cuts and bruises, but Art was not so lucky. He was left with horrific injuries – injuries that included a broken neck. The doctors managed to save his life, but there was nothing they could do to repair the injuries to his spinal cord. At the age of 21 Art found himself a quadriplegic, paralysed from the neck down.

It is almost impossible for most of us to imagine how that would feel. Faced with a similar situation many people would be hard pushed to find the courage to go on living. But somehow Art not only found the courage to go on living, he also found a new sense of purpose in defying the people who told him that he could not do things. His doctors told him that he was a quadriplegic. He refused to accept this diagnosis. To their astonishment he regained significant use of one arm and partial use of the other. His doctors told him he would be confined to an electric wheelchair for the rest of his life. He pushed himself out of hospital in a manual one just four months later. His physiotherapist told him he would never be able to dress himself again. It took him five years, but he got there.

During the following 19 years Art Berg:

- won three national awards as a computer salesman
- was named Utah Young Entrepreneur of the Year 1992
- set up his own public-speaking company, which involved travelling more than 200,000 miles per year
- wrote three bestselling books
- completed a 325-mile wheelchair ultra-marathon race across the Utah desert
- went scuba diving with his friends
- married his fiancée and adopted two children with her

I was very sorry to hear that Art Berg died in February 2002 from an adverse reaction to medication. His life could so easily have been a tragedy, but it was not. His achievements during the last 19 years of his life will live on as an inspiration to us all.

Now look again at that list you just wrote of the obstacles that you thought might stop you from achieving your dreams. With Art's story fresh in your mind, let's have a look at how you might be able to overcome these little difficulties.

CHAPTER 8

If you don't know how

*'I'd love to be an astronaut/football player/pop star,
but I just don't know where to begin.'*

If you repeat this phrase to yourself often enough you will convince yourself that it is true and it will become a self-fulfilling prophecy.

If you want to do something and don't know where to begin, the solution can be summed up in five words:

Find someone who does know.

Whatever it is that you want to do, someone will have done it (or something like it) before. If you can find out how they went about achieving their success, you will be in a much better position to emulate their achievements.

Let's imagine, for example, that your ambition is to become the heavyweight boxing champion of the world. You might start by buying some biographies or, better still, autobiographies of some of the former champions like Muhammad Ali, Henry Cooper and Lennox Lewis. Your objective in reading these books is not to learn to box – that's best done in the gym. What you need to find out is what motivated them to become world champion. How did they get their first break? What sacrifices did they have to make along the way? Their psychology is just as important as their skills.

For this reason it is important to read as many different biographies about the same person as possible. Each one will give you new insights and new perspectives, and the more you know, the better equipped you will be to find your own route to success.

Next you might do an internet search for articles about all the former champions. If you don't have access to a computer, go to your local library or to an internet café. Print off as many articles as you can. This type of research is like peeling an onion – there's always another layer to discover underneath. Find out what films have been made about the former champions and try to see as many of them as possible. They will often tell Hollywood's 'sanitised' version of real events, but they will still give you useful background knowledge.

Once you have found out all you can from public sources, you could draw up a list of the living champions whom you would most like to meet and the questions you would most like to ask them. Turn these questions into a short letter. Now why not send it to them? I am quite serious. In my experience people who have reached the very top of their fields are often very willing to help others on their way and the advice that they give you and the very fact that they took the time out to reply could have an enormous impact on your future success. Even a reply from one of their aides could be useful and motivational.

Your ultimate goal, however, should be a meeting. There is something magical about a face-to-face meeting, however brief, which cannot be achieved in any other way. It might be easier to arrange than you think. Look on the internet to see if any of your role models are due to speak at a public event in the future. If they are, do whatever it takes to get a front-row seat. If none of your role models speaks in public, find some others who do, or perhaps try for a meeting with one of their aides. Every scrap of knowledge that you glean will help you along the way to realising your dream.

The effectiveness of this process is something that I can testify to from my own experience. I remember very clearly the day that I decided to set up my charitable trust to take my message to teenagers. It was July 2000, and a delegate on a course that I had run in Southampton had just spent ten minutes telling me how much he wished that he had had an opportunity to attend my course 20 years earlier when he was still at school. A great many other people had said the same thing to me before, but for some reason this chap really touched a nerve.

I spent the whole journey home thinking about what he had said. By the time I reached the M25 I had decided that I had to set up a foundation to make my material available to young people. At the time I don't think I had spoken to a teenager for 20 years! I did not have the faintest idea about how I was going to adapt my seminar to suit a younger audience and just for a moment I caught myself thinking, 'I could never do that. I don't know where to begin.' As soon as I realised what I was thinking, I laughed and said out loud, 'Then you must find someone who does know.'

I started by looking at Amazon, the online bookshop, and I ordered a couple of dozen books on careers advice and goal-planning for young people. Next I commissioned an internet researcher to find out about other people who spoke on the subject and what was happening in UK schools at the moment. I found that most of the work that had been done in this area had been done in the United States, so I booked myself a place on a week-long camp that taught American teenagers exactly the sort of skills that I wanted to teach. While I was there I made a point of talking to as many people as I could about my plans to do something similar in the UK. I managed to talk to all the main speakers and I received an enormous amount of encouragement and practical advice.

A teacher from Arizona called Manny Leybas, who has been teaching goal-setting to his pupils for ten years, gave me his top tip for keeping his audiences interested. 'Pick a row of ten people at random,' he said. 'If more than three of them aren't paying attention then you need to change the subject immediately.' It was a wonderful piece of advice that I have used many times since.

An educational psychologist called Dr Larry Martell told me how to use videos and other visual aids to increase a young audience's attention span. His advice, which is based on meticulous scientific research, is so simple that it can be summed up in a sentence: 'You can't expect people to pay attention 100 per cent of the time, so leave a video running in the corner of the room to occupy them during these moments of inattention.' Applying this advice had an immediate effect on my audiences' attentiveness.

But the most useful piece of advice of all came from a speaker called Marlon Smith. Marlon is president of an organisation called Success by Choice and he speaks to young people all over the world. I had not heard of Marlon before I attended the camp and I missed his speech because it clashed with another speaker I wanted to hear in an adjacent hall. Within moments of sitting down to dinner that evening I knew that missing Marlon's speech had been a mistake. The young people at my table who had heard him speak were simply buzzing with excitement. They agreed unanimously that he was the best speaker of the entire week. I thought to myself, 'This is someone I just have to meet.'

The very next day I sought Marlon out and introduced myself. I told him that the students had all agreed that his session was the best of the week. I asked him for more details of what he had spoken about and told him a little about my work in the UK. We spoke for only about ten minutes, but I felt an immediate connection with him and gave him my address and contact details for the future.

Two months later I received a phone call. Marlon was passing through the UK *en route* to South Africa and wanted to know if I would like to meet up for the day. 'What a fantastic opportunity to spend a whole day with one of the best speakers in the world,' I thought. I met Marlon at Heathrow Airport at 7 a.m. on a Monday. He had just completed a nine-hour overnight flight from the United States and had another nine-hour flight to take that evening. It wouldn't have been fair of me to spend the entire day bombarding him with questions, so we had a pleasant day sightseeing and chatting about things in general.

Over dinner that evening the time finally seemed right to ask Marlon the question that I had been waiting to ask all day. 'Marlon,' I said, 'what advice would you give an experienced business speaker on how to adapt his material for a younger audience?'

His reply surprised me. 'Adam,' he said, 'what you need to bear in mind is that with a younger audience the day will be won or lost before you have even said good morning. My advice to you would be to invest in the best audio-visual equipment that you can afford and prepare a fabulous audio-visual presentation to start the day off with a bang.' Then he changed the subject.

Again, the advice was so simple that it could be summed up in a sentence, but I knew instinctively that Marlon was right. I followed his advice to the letter and spent thousands of pounds on buying a new sound system and a state-of-the-art projector to ensure that the day really did start with a bang. With hindsight I can see that this was undoubtedly the key factor behind the success of my early seminars.

The lessons that I learned from Manny Leybas, Larry Martell and Marlon Smith were all very simple ones. But they were lessons that could have been taught to me only by people who had spent many years working their way up to the very top of their chosen fields. I could have learned these lessons the hard way, but what a terrible waste of my time and resources that would have been.

In a world that is so full of knowledge there can be no excuse. If you don't know how to do something, find someone who does.

CHAPTER 9

If you fear others' reactions

'You'll never do that.'
'Don't be so stupid.'
'Just who do you think you are?'

How many times have your friends and family shot down your dreams with comments like these? In a moment we will look at what you can do to maintain your motivation in the face of such criticism. But before we do so, it might be helpful to understand why so many people are so negative about the dreams of others.

Some are just jealous – inwardly they don't really want to see you succeed. Others (and this tends to be particularly true of parents) are trying to protect you from the disappointment that they see as inevitable. However, by far the biggest reason behind most people's hostility is fear. They are frightened that if you achieve your dreams you will be better than they are and won't want to spend time with them any more. Once you know this you will start to see their hostility and negativity in a completely different light. Rather than taking their comments seriously, you can just quietly pity them for their insecurity. There is no point arguing with people like this. You are very unlikely to persuade them to be more supportive, and the energy that you expend trying would usually be better spent working towards achieving your goals.

Dealing with negative comments

When you get negative comments about your plans, the best strategy is usually to change the subject as quickly as possible in order to minimise the damage to your self-confidence.

If you fear that a negative comment has had an effect on your morale, you should read through your goals again as soon as possible.

- Remind yourself why you must achieve this goal. Remind yourself what it would cost you and the people you care about if you didn't achieve this goal.

- Reassure yourself that your strategies for achieving your goals are still sound.

- Look at all the milestones that you have already achieved and remind yourself that it would be a shame to give up now.

This technique should quickly restore your motivation and self-belief.

However, a better strategy still might be to try to avoid putting yourself in this situation in the first place. If you know that a certain friend or family member is likely to be negative about your future plans, it might be best all round if you kept your plans to yourself in future. I'll go further. If a particular friend is consistently negative about your future plans, you might even question what purpose their friendship serves and reconsider whether you need that person in your life at all.

Getting support

While negative people can sap your morale, positive people can have a hugely beneficial effect on it. Peer pressure is enormously powerful. As the old adage goes, 'Who you spend time with is who you become.'

Your chances of achieving your dreams will be increased

exponentially if you can surround yourself with energetic, positive, supportive people.

Take a moment now to list in your notebook the names of all the people you know who can be relied upon to support you wholeheartedly in everything that you seek to achieve.

If there are fewer than ten names on this list you might want to spend some time thinking about what you could do to meet some more supportive and positive people. This is so important that some radical action might be necessary.

- Should you take up a new hobby?

- Should you move house?

- Should you change your job?

Remember, who you spend time with is who you become. Think about the people you spend most of your time with now and ask yourself honestly, 'Is this who I want to become in five or ten years' time?'

Take a few moments to think about what changes may be necessary here before you move on to the next chapter.

CHAPTER 10

If you fear making mistakes

I'd like to tell you the story of two famous people, a writer and a sportsman. The writer's name is J. D. Salinger and he is best known for writing *The Catcher in the Rye*, which he wrote when he was just 26 years old. When I tell this story in my seminars, I ask if anyone can remember the title of his second book. No one ever can. J. D. Salinger has reputedly written many more novels during the last 58 years, but with the exception of some short stories, he has never submitted anything for publication. The reason? Apparently he is worried that they might be judged to be not as good as the first one!

Now contrast this with the story of a really terrible basketball player. He was so bad that he *missed* nearly 100,000 shots during his professional career. His name was Michael Jordan, and despite making more than 100,000 'mistakes' in full view of millions of his fans, he still got enough shots in to become the greatest basketball player the world has ever known.

Making mistakes is normal, healthy and an essential part of the learning process. We all know this. So why then are so many people so frightened of making even the tiniest error?

Perfectionist behaviour

The answer lies back in childhood. People who fear making mistakes learn this behaviour early. What they usually have in common is a parent who was judgemental, critical and hard to please and whose love seemed conditional, tied to things such as how well they performed or how good or capable they were.

For a small child, parental approval is essential. Without it they could quite literally die. By making this approval conditional on behaviour, such parents are unwittingly setting up perfectionist behaviour patterns which will have consequences throughout the whole of their children's lives.

Perfectionist behaviour can manifest itself in a number of different ways:

- Many people fear making errors or wrong decisions. Some become so preoccupied with making the right choice every time that they have difficulty making even relatively simple decisions such as where to go on holiday or what dish to choose from a restaurant menu.

- Some people become finicky over minor details to such an extent that their pleasure is spoiled unless everything is just so.

- Some people spend hours worrying about making the right decision or ruminating over decisions that have already been made.

- Some people become workaholics because they waste hours polishing even the most inconsequential piece of work.

- Some people become so intent on finding the ultimate romantic partner that they become unable to commit to any long-term relationship.

- Some people procrastinate over decisions to such an extent that the decision ends up being made for them.

- Some people become obsessively tidy.

- Some people cannot bear to be criticised.

The consequences of such behaviour can be disastrous. Not only will they prevent you from achieving your goals, but left unchecked, they will drive away the people you care about, rob you of your health and deprive you of any sense of fulfilment from your accomplishments. So what can be done?

CHANGING PERFECTIONIST BEHAVIOUR

I'd like you to start by listing all the perfectionist behaviour that you would like to change, for example, excessive tidiness, procrastination, rumination, workaholism, perfectionism over work, fear of making mistakes, etc.

Now work through this eight-stage process with each of the unwanted forms of behaviour in turn.

- What is the behaviour that I want to change?

    – For example, procrastinating over making decisions.

- What has this behaviour cost me so far?

    – Hours of pointless worrying about the most minor decisions.

    – Having to buy my second choice of car because the old one broke down before I'd finished deciding what to buy and my first choice wasn't available at short notice.

    – Loss of a Christmas holiday last year because by the time I had made a decision as to where I wanted to go, all the flights were full.

- What could this behaviour cost me in the future?

    – The respect of my family.

    – My own self-respect.

    – Wasted business opportunities.

    – Thousands more pointless hours wasted on making the most minor decisions.

- What has this behaviour already cost the people I care about?

  – The kids were so disappointed about the Christmas holiday.

- What could this behaviour cost the people I care about in the future?

  – More missed holidays.

  – More time spent with an irritable father/husband.

- Why must I change this behaviour?.

  – Because it will cost me my self-respect.

  – Because it will cost me the respect of my family.

  – Because I deserve more.

  – Because continuing to behave like this will cost me my destiny.

- What specific actions can I take to change this behaviour?

  – Make all future decisions on paper rather than in my head.

  – Set a deadline for making each new decision.

  – If the deadline passes, flip a coin to decide.

  – List the worst possible consequences of making the wrong decision. Stick them on the wall and remind myself that none of these is as bad as the awful process of procrastination itself.

- How can I reward myself for changing this behaviour?

  – When I make my next decision within the self-imposed deadline, I will treat myself to a day go-kart racing.

Repeat this process with any other behaviour that you want to change, and monitor the situation closely for the next three months. Many people are pleasantly surprised at how easy it is to change behaviour that has handicapped them for years.

CHAPTER 11

If you lack confidence

'You'll never do that.'
'You are such an idiot.'
'You stupid imbecile.'

If someone consistently speaks to you like this, you should, as I said earlier, consider cutting that person out of your life permanently. But what if you yourself are the abuser? Most of us have a little voice in our head that bombards us with insults like this day after day. This sort of negative self-talk can be hugely damaging. If you are serious about achieving your goals, you are going to have to do something about it.

LISTENING TO YOUR INNER VOICE

I would like you to start by writing down everything that your inner voice says to you on a regular basis.

- What does it say when you have just made a mistake? 'You idiot'?

- What does it say when it wants to stop you from trying something new? 'You'll never do that'?

- What negative questions does it ask you day after day? 'Why are you so stupid?'?

Take a few minutes to write down all the negative things that your inner voice says to you.

Now read through that list again. Read each of those negative things out loud. Do so with real emotion in your voice.

How does that feel? Pretty demoralising I should expect. And yet you say these same things to yourself day after day, week after week, year after year. No wonder you lack confidence. This needs to be addressed, doesn't it? But how?

The key is to understand that what you say to yourself is not nearly as important as *how* you say it. Let me show you what I mean.

- Take the most damaging thing that your inner voice says to you.

- Now think of the silliest voice that you can think of – a Donald Duck-type voice perhaps, or a very high-pitched voice, or one that speaks with a very silly accent. Use your imagination. Think of the silliest voice that you can.

- Now take the most damaging thing that your inner voice says to you and say it to yourself again in that ridiculous voice. Say it again and again. Say it out loud. Say it ten more times.

How does that feel? Does your inner voice have the same power to demoralise you when it is forced to speak like this? I doubt it very much. This might seem like a bizarre technique, but many people find it to be remarkably effective. Try it next time you catch that inner voice trying to demoralise you.

Negative beliefs

However, the problem for some people is that their negative voice has been demoralising them for years. If this is so, no motivational technique will be able to reverse overnight the damage that has been done over many years. If, for example, you have spent the last ten years telling yourself that you are stupid, part of you will have come to believe that this is true.

Most of us have a number of negative beliefs about ourselves. Sometimes we are not even fully aware of them consciously and yet they can have a huge effect upon our level of motivation, our ability to achieve and our sense of happiness and well-being.

DISCOVERING YOUR NEGATIVE BELIEFS

So what negative beliefs do you have about yourself? What do you believe about yourself when you are feeling really low? Do you ever catch yourself thinking 'I could never do this' or 'I'm not the sort of person who does that'?

- Take a few moments to pick up your notebook and write down all the negative or limiting beliefs that you have about yourself.

- Now what do you believe about other people when you are feeling low? For example, 'Most people are cleverer than me,' or 'Most people don't like me.' Take a moment to write down all the negative and limiting beliefs that you have about other people.

- Finally, write down what you believe about the world when you are feeling low. For example, 'Life is always so unfair.' Take a moment to write down all the beliefs that you have about society or the world in general.

- Now look at those beliefs in the cold light of day. Are they true? Are you really stupid? Is it really true that most people don't like you? Is life always unfair? Of course not. It's just that damned inner voice speaking again, isn't it?

- So put yourself in a more positive frame of mind. Think back to a time when you were being yourself at your very best. And in that strong, positive frame of mind, go back through the years and compile a list of all the things you've done that have made you feel really proud. Do this before you read on.

- Now read through that list two or three times. Read each achievement out loud to yourself in a strong, proud voice, a voice that really does justice to each of your achievements.

- Now, still in that strong, positive frame of mind, look again at that list of negative beliefs. Read each in turn and write a more accurate belief next to it. For example, if your old disempowering belief was 'I could never do something like that', your new empowering belief might be 'I can do anything that I set my mind to'.

- When you have finished, read through each pair of beliefs out loud. In a silly high-pitched voice say, 'I used to believe that I could never do something like that,' then cross that old belief out. Change the tone of your voice and with real power and authority say, 'That's nonsense. The truth is I can do anything that I set my mind to.'

- Some people like to make a poster of their new empowering beliefs and display it on the wall. Some people even find it helpful to burn their old list of limiting beliefs. This helps to signify that they really have left them behind for ever.

- Finally, combine the two parts of the exercise. Read through your list of positive references in a strong, positive voice. Then read your list of new empowering beliefs in a confident, authoritative tone.

How is your confidence now? Do you feel certain that you will achieve your goals? You can repeat this exercise again and again whenever you feel your confidence is flagging.

CHAPTER 12

If you lack motivation

However exciting your goals are, there will inevitably be times when you just don't feel like working towards achieving them. This feeling can be summed up by the diagram overleaf.

You know the result that you are trying to achieve, for example a healthy body. You also know exactly what you need to do in order to achieve it, for example eat healthily, exercise and sleep. So what stops you? Well, what stops you are your own emotions. When you feel happy or excited, you have no difficulty whatsoever finding the motivation to work towards achieving your goals. But when you feel sad, it's so very easy to flop in front of the television all day or seek solace in junk food.

So the next question to ask must be: what controls your emotions? The answer is that *you* do – at least you could if you knew how to.

Most people believe that their moods are wholly beyond their control. This is simply not true. In order to feel a certain way you have to do a number of very specific things. Once you know what they are, you will find that you are able to change the way that you feel in a moment.

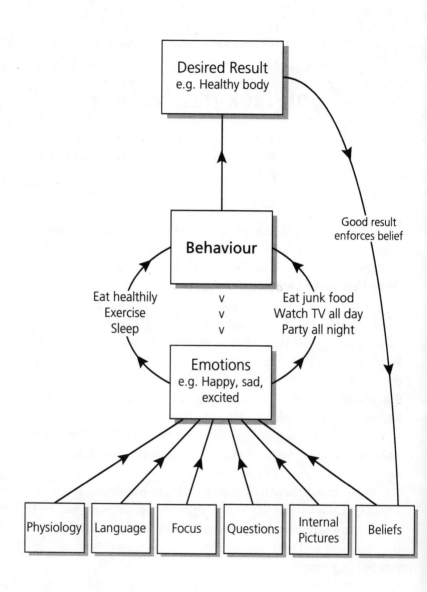

The easiest way for me to demonstrate this is with an exercise. This particular exercise will be much easier to do if you can find someone to help you. You don't need to share your innermost secrets with them; you just need someone who can read the exercise to you, observe what you are doing and write it down. I will assume from this point onwards that you have found someone to help you. If you really can't find anyone, you will just have to do the best you can to write down what you did from memory.

Give this book to your partner and ask them to read the exercise to you. They will need a pen and paper to record your responses. There is a 'Personal Strategy for Success' chart below that they can copy and fill in.

Your Personal Strategy for Success

Disempowering	*Empowering*
Physiology	
Eyes down	Eyes up

Language	
I should	I must
I'll try	I will

Focus	
My last failure	My last success

Questions	
What if I fail?	How will I enjoy my success?

chart continues

Beliefs	
I can't do this	I'm good at this

Internal Pictures	
Number of images:	
Colour/Black and white:	
Bright/Dim:	
In focus/Out of focus:	
Shape:	
Size in relation to real life:	
Bordered/Panoramic:	
3D/Flat:	
Close/Far away:	
In motion/Still:	
Are you in the picture?:	
Location in space:	
Further reading:	

Used with written permission from Dr Richard Bandler, 2004.

chart continues

EXERCISE *(to be read to you by a partner)*

- I'd like you to close your eyes and remember a time when you were finding it very difficult to motivate yourself to do something. Put yourself into the state of mind that you were in then. See what you saw, hear what you heard, say what you said to yourself.

- Now stand the way you stand when you really can't find the motivation to do something. *(Partner: record how they are standing on left-hand side of chart.)*

- Now say what you say to yourself when you really can't find the motivation to do something. *(Partner: record this on chart too.)*

- Now think about what you focus on when you really can't find the motivation to do something. Do you focus on your last success or your last failure? Do you focus on how easy the task will be or how difficult? *(Partner: record this on chart too.)*

- Now while you are still in that disempowering state of being unable to find the motivation to do something, ask yourself the questions that you ask yourself. Are they positive questions like 'How good will I feel when I've done this?' or are they negative questions like 'What if I fail?'? *(Partner: record their answers.)*

- Now what do you believe when you really can't find the motivation to do something? Do you have negative beliefs like 'I can't do this' or 'The whole world is against me'? *(Partner: record this.)*

- Finally, while you are still in that unmotivated state, I'd like you to create a picture in your mind of the thing that you really can't find the motivation to do. How does that picture look? Is it colour or black and white? Is it bright or dim? Is it in focus or out of focus? What shape is it? How big is it, relative to real life? Is it bordered or panoramic? Is it 3D or flat? Is it close to you or far away? Is it a motion picture or a still picture? Can you see yourself in the picture? Now point to where that picture is in space. *(Partner: record their answers to each of these questions in detail.)*

- Now open your eyes and shake yourself out of that disempowering state and return to a neutral mood. (Some people find that it takes a few minutes to do this.)

- Now close your eyes again and remember a time when you couldn't wait to do something. Think of a time when you were so motivated to do something that you were tingling with excitement. Now stand the way that you would stand when you are really motivated to do something. Breathe the way you would breathe when you are really motivated to do something. *(Partner: record how they are standing on right-hand side of chart.)*

- Now say what you say to yourself when you are really motivated to do something. *(Partner: write this down.)*

- Now focus on what you focus on when you are really motivated to do something. *(Partner: write this down.)*

- Now ask the questions that you ask yourself when you are really motivated to do something. *(Partner: write these down.)*

- Now what do you believe when you are really motivated to do something? What do you believe about yourself? What do you believe about others? What do you believe about the world? *(Partner: write this down.)*

- Finally, make the picture that you make when you are really motivated to do something, the picture that you make when you are so excited that you just can't wait to get started. *(Partner: record this in detail.)* How does that picture look? Is it in colour or black and white? Is it bright or dim? Is it in focus or out of focus? What shape is it? How big is it, relative to real life? Is it bordered or panoramic? Is it 3D or flat? Is it close to you or far away? Is it a motion picture or a still picture? Can you see yourself in the picture? Now point to where that picture is in space. *(Partner: record their answers to each of these questions in detail.)*

- Now enjoy that feeling for just a moment longer, then, when you are ready, open your eyes, feeling great.

Now compare the notes that your partner has made in the left and the right columns. Are they very different? I would be astonished if they weren't.

Most people believe that because they feel miserable they look down at the floor, hunch their shoulders forward, let their muscles go slack and stop breathing properly. Let me tell you something amazing: it doesn't work like this. It actually works the other way round. You don't adopt poor physiology because you feel miserable, you feel miserable because you adopt poor physiology.

Once you know this, you can change the way that you feel in an instant. Let me prove this to you with the second part of this exercise. (This part too is much easier to do with a partner.)

- I'd like you to think of something that you are finding it difficult to find the motivation to do. Close your eyes and create an image of it in your mind. Then have your partner read you the following instructions. They will need the 'Personal Strategy for Success' chart that they have just completed ready to hand.

- With the image of the thing that you really can't find the motivation to do clearly in your mind, I'd like you to stand the way you would stand when you feel really motivated to do something. I'd like you to breathe the way you would breathe when you can't wait to do something. Stand up straight, pull your shoulders right back and . . . *(Partner: read them all the empowering things that they do with their physiology from their own chart.)*

- Now with the image of whatever you can't find the motivation to do still in your mind, I'd like you to say what you say to yourself when you can't wait to start something. 'I must do it.' 'I will do it.' *(Partner: read them all their own phrases from their chart.)*

- Now with the image of the thing that you used not to have the motivation to do clearly in your mind, focus on what you would focus on if you did have the motivation to do it. *(Partner: read them their own strategies.)*

- Now with that image still in your mind, ask yourself the questions that you would ask if you had the motivation to start it immediately. For example . . . *(Partner: read them their own empowering questions.)*

- Now with that image still in your mind, think about what you would believe if you really had the motivation to start it immediately. For example . . . *(Partner: read them their own empowering beliefs.)*

- Finally I'd like you to make a picture of that thing you once didn't have the motivation to do. Make it in colour. Make it brighter. Make it more in focus. *(Partner: read them their own empowering picture formula from their sheet.)*

- Now when you have that picture exactly the way you want it, I'd like you to step into the picture and, as you do so, know that you have achieved your goal.

- Now enjoy that feeling of excitement and fulfilment for one last moment, then open your eyes, feeling great.

How do you feel now about that thing that you know you should do? Rather more motivated to tackle it? You can repeat this exercise whenever you need to motivate yourself to do something. Once you understand how your own personal strategy for success works, you will be able to change the way that you feel in a moment and be at your very best whenever you need to.

This goes to the very heart of what personal development is all about. By finding out what you do when you are performing at your very best, you will find that you are able to achieve outstanding results much more consistently. As you become more aware of how to communicate with yourself through your physiology, through the language you use and through the images you create in your own mind, you will find that you become able to transfer positive emotions such as confidence and certainty to new situations.

If you approach a new situation with greater confidence, you will achieve better results, and these results will in turn have an impact on your beliefs. With your self-belief newly reinforced, you will adopt even better physiology, use even more positive language, ask yourself even better questions and create even more empowering images. With even greater confidence you will find yourself able to achieve even more outstanding results. Which, in turn, will reinforce your beliefs.

Thus a virtuous circle is created. Each new success will improve your confidence, and your increased confidence will enable you to achieve even greater success.

CHAPTER 13

Setbacks beyond your control

However meticulously you plan your goals, you will, sooner or later, encounter a setback that is entirely beyond your control. A good example of this from my own life would be the series of setbacks that I encountered when I was setting up the Adam Walker Foundation. These included:

- The Charity Commission refused to allow me to register as a charity on the grounds that personal development was not a charitable purpose in law.

- Because of the Charity Commission's decision, the sponsorship deal that I had negotiated with a major UK insurance company was withdrawn.

- The public-relations company that had promised me national publicity for my first seminar failed to deliver.

As a result of these unexpected setbacks I lost more than £50,000 promoting my first public seminar. But I didn't mind. I was doing something that I believed in and I felt sure that if I persevered, I would recover my financial losses in due course. And then came the final blow.

Just as I was about to make the seminar available to secondary schools throughout the country, the Government changed the examination process by introducing the now infamous AS levels. Suddenly, Year 12 pupils were faced with such a barrage of new examinations that there was no time left in the curriculum for anything else. I offered my seminar to more than 2,500 secondary schools and did not receive a single positive response. After two years' planning and a £50,000 investment, the whole project lay in ruins.

I cursed the new examination system and the Minister for Education who had introduced it. The new AS levels were deeply unpopular with both teachers and students and I was very tempted to join the campaign for a return to the old system. However, on reflection I realised that it was quite beyond my power to influence government policy and that my time and energy would be much better spent working on the things that I *could* control. What I did instead was what I always do when I am faced with a major challenge: I sat down and reread some of my favourite personal-development books. The book that I turned to first was *Man's Search for Meaning* by Viktor Frankl.

Viktor Frankl was a survivor of the Holocaust. He wrote his book immediately upon his release from Auschwitz. During the three years that he spent there he witnessed unimaginable acts of cruelty and humiliation. But Dr Frankl was no ordinary prisoner. Before his incarceration he had trained as a psychiatrist and, despite his own pain and suffering, he became fascinated by how his fellow prisoners responded to their situation. Why, he wondered, did some prisoners sink immediately into a black pit of despair while others kept their hope alive? Why did some fight with their fellow prisoners like animals while others would willingly share their last crust of bread with someone who was even worse off than they were? His conclusion was that even when a man has had every last thing taken from him, he still has one last freedom left – the freedom to choose his own response. And so could I. I could choose to respond to a serious setback by giving up on a project that was very dear to my heart or I could find another way. I knew what I had to do.

I sat down with a clean sheet of paper and I asked myself, 'What is my ultimate outcome for the Adam Walker Foundation?' The answer was: 'I want to introduce young people to the benefits of personal-development techniques *before* they waste years climbing the ladder of success only to find that it was leaning against entirely the wrong wall. I also want to make goal-setting, personal development and work/life balance compulsory topics within the national curriculum.'

Next I asked myself, 'What areas are entirely within my power to change?' The answer was: 'The format and style of my seminar.'

Finally, I asked myself, 'How else could I achieve my ultimate outcome?' The answer was: 'I could make my seminar available on video.' Instead of running it as a full day's session I could redesign it as eight 45-minute sessions which teachers could use in the weekly Personal Health and Social Development lesson (which became a compulsory part of the school curriculum from September 2002).

And that is exactly what I did. The video, entitled *Succeed for Yourself*, is being shot as this book goes to press. And my intention is to make a copy of it available to every UK secondary school.

So there's your process. If you encounter a setback that is quite beyond your control:

- Choose your response.

- Focus your time and energy on the things that you *can* control.

- Focus on your ultimate outcome.

- Be flexible about the strategies that you employ to achieve it.

CHAPTER 14

Learning from failure

Most books on goal-setting don't include a section on failure. Their authors would argue that any mention of the word 'failure' is defeatist, and suggest instead that you repeat the mantra 'There is always a way'. However, in the real world it is highly probable that you will, at some point, fail to achieve a goal, and I feel that this book would be incomplete without a section on what to do when this happens.

Essentially there are two reasons for not achieving a goal:

- The goal no longer seems important to you.

- You are unable to overcome an obstacle to success.

Let's look at each of these in turn.

Experiencing a change of heart

Just occasionally you will set yourself a goal and then later, perhaps in the light of experience, decide that achieving this goal is no longer important to you. When this occurs it is very important to be sure that your change of heart is genuine rather than just an excuse for giving up on a goal that has become too difficult to achieve. Your goals should not be set in stone. However, it is all too easy to get into the habit of excusing every failure by saying to yourself, 'Well, I didn't really want to do that anyway.'

The best way to analyse how genuine your reasons are is to put them down in writing. (It's much harder to lie to yourself on paper.)

If, in the light of this, you realise your change of heart is not genuine, go back and read Chapters 7–13 again to help you overcome any obstacles in your path. If your change of mind is genuine, then record the reason for it in your notebook, cross the goal out and think of a new one to put in its place.

Experiencing failure

But what if you can't achieve a goal that is still important to you? I am not being defeatist here – there sometimes comes a point where the mantra 'There is always a way' no longer rings true. If this happens to you it is essential that you do three things:

1. Ask yourself the right questions.

2. Attribute the right meaning to your setback.

3. Learn useful lessons for the future.

Let me show you what I mean. Suppose, for example, that your goal was to climb the Matterhorn. You spent months preparing yourself for the climb and four days fighting your way up to the top. But when you were less than 500 metres from the summit, disaster struck. The weather broke and you realised that it would be suicidal to press on. With great reluctance you were forced to abandon the climb. Let's look at how you might deal with this sort of failure.

The first essential would be to ask yourself the right questions. You might ask yourself questions like:

- Why do I always give up on everything that I attempt? (Because I'm a dismal failure.)

- Why did the weather have to break? (Because God doesn't think I deserved to succeed.)
- Why didn't I spend my money on a holiday with my family in Hawaii instead of wasting it pursuing such a hopeless dream? (Because I am a stupid, selfish person.)

You see what I mean – if you ask stupid questions, the little voice in your head will give you stupid answers.

So what positive questions could you ask yourself in this situation? You might ask instead:

- What did I learn from this experience?
- How can I use what I have learned to be more successful in other areas of my life?
- What part of the experience did I really enjoy?

Better questions produce better answers and make you feel so much better about any experience.

The second essential is to attach the right meaning to your setback. You cannot change the fact that you have failed to climb the Matterhorn. However, you can decide what that setback means to you. If you decide that it means you are a hopeless individual who gives up on everything, your failed attempt will have a negative effect on your future life. If you decide that the decision to give up at the right point was a testament to your good judgement and represents the love that you feel for your family, you will feel much better about the whole experience.

I find that many people attach negative meanings to their experiences subconsciously. The best way to prevent this is actually to write down the meanings that you would like to attach to each situation.

Finally, you need to ask yourself the question, 'What can I learn from this setback?' Sometimes achieving a goal is less important than what you learned and who you become along the way.

I can't close this chapter without making another reference to

Art Berg whom I first mentioned in Chapter 7. As a young man of 21 Art Berg once had the goal of building a successful business constructing tennis courts. His accident prevented him from achieving this, of course. But because he asked the right questions and attributed the right meanings, just look at the triumph that his life became instead.

PART FOUR

Finding true fulfilment

CHAPTER 15

Maintaining the
work/life balance

We all have periods when we have to devote a disproportionate amount of our time to achieving results in just one area of our lives. For example, if you have just started a business it would be perfectly appropriate to spend most of your time getting it off the ground. If you have just had your first child, it would be essential to make its well-being your priority during the first crucial year of its life. However, if you focus on just one area of your life for too long, you will, almost inevitably, become deeply unhappy.

Whenever I talk about the work/life balance I am reminded of one of my clients, let's call him Harry, who paid a particularly heavy price for allowing his life to become out of balance. Harry was the managing director of a company that I prepared a business plan for about five years ago. The business plan was an ambitious one – his goal was to treble the size of his business within five years – and Harry and his team knew that a lot of hard work would be required to achieve their outcome. Their business plan was a wonderful success, such a success in fact that they achieved their goal within two years rather than five.

Harry and his team had a huge party to celebrate their achievement. But Harry's happiness was to be short-lived. Just a few days after the party his wife told him that she was having an affair with another man. Harry was absolutely devastated. In his eyes he had worked 18 hours a day, seven days a week, for two whole years in order to provide a stable financial future for his family. But his wife didn't see things that way. In her eyes he had simply lost interest in her and the children. As a result she had started an affair with a man who had more time for her.

This is not a story with a happy ending. Harry could not forgive his wife for her infidelity and she could not forgive him for his 'lack of interest'. They were forced to accept that their marriage had broken down irreversibly and Harry left the family home for ever. What a tragedy – a marriage destroyed, four young children deprived of their father and the family's finances devastated. And the story doesn't end there. The final irony is that Harry was so badly affected by the breakdown of his marriage that he was unable to concentrate on his work. Within 18 months his business got into serious financial difficulties and he was forced to sell it to a competitor. Today Harry lives alone in a small flat and struggles to pay the cost of running two homes on a salary that is a fraction of what he used to earn.

So what can be learned from this story? Well, it was perfectly appropriate for Harry to make expanding his business his prime area of focus for a time. But when his work started to occupy every waking moment and the months turned into years, he should have realised that his life was out of balance. But of course he didn't, because the situation just crept up on him day by day. Now, with hindsight, Harry realises that no amount of business success could ever make up for the family that he has lost.

How many people do you know who have made similar mistakes to Harry? How many people do you know who have achieved success in one area of their lives only by sacrificing something that was far more important? And how can you avoid making similar mistakes?

HOW BALANCED IS YOUR LIFE?

Here's an exercise to do to check how balanced your life is currently. Using the same ten categories that I introduced in Chapter 3, I would like you to give yourself a score out of ten for how satisfied you feel with each of the main areas of your life.

- Start with the financial category. On a scale of 1–10, how satisfied do you feel with what you have achieved financially? If you are living comfortably within your means and feel that you have already achieved your full financial potential, give yourself a 10. If you are up to your ears in debt and feel that you are worth far more than you are currently paid, give yourself a 1. If you feel that your financial position is midway between the two, then give yourself a 5. Don't agonise over what to put. This exercise works best if it is done quickly.

- Now move on to how satisfied you feel with your career. If you are in a job that you love and have already achieved your full career potential, give yourself a 10. If you are in a job that you loathe and have just been passed over for promotion for the tenth time, give yourself a 1. If you feel that your current situation is somewhere between the two extremes, give yourself the appropriate score.

- Now move on to how stretched you currently feel intellectually. If your current job and/or hobbies stretch you to your intellectual limits on a daily basis, give yourself a 10. If you can't remember the last time that you asked your brain to solve a new problem, give yourself a 1. Otherwise, give yourself an appropriate score between the two.

- Next move on to your physical health. If you love the way you look, eat only wholesome healthy food, exercise every day and are bursting with health and vitality during every waking moment, give yourself a 10 (remember it's important to do this exercise truthfully!). If you are twice your ideal weight, eat nothing but junk food and haven't done a day's exercise since you left school, give yourself a 1. Otherwise, give yourself an appropriate score between the two.

- Now ask yourself how fulfilled you feel emotionally. If your current life regularly fills you with a deep sense of joy and fulfilment, give yourself a 10. If your life is dominated by unresolved issues from your childhood, if you are plagued by unresolved feelings of guilt, anger or resentment, or if you suffer from depression or an eating disorder, give yourself a 1. If the truth lies somewhere between the two, give yourself whatever score feels right for you.

- Think next about your close relationships. How do you get on with your partner, your children and your parents? If these key relationships are filled with love, trust and mutual respect, give yourself a 10. If you are on the brink of divorce and are no longer on speaking terms with either your children or your parents, give yourself a 1. Otherwise, give yourself whatever score seems right to you.

- Now think about your home. If you love the place that you live in, give yourself a 10. If you are sharing a tiny flat on a sink council estate with six flatmates from hell, give yourself a 1. Otherwise, give yourself the appropriate mark between the two.

- Next move on to consider your social life. If you have a wide circle of wonderful friends and have a great time out with them on a regular basis, give yourself a 10. If you have just one or two close friends and really enjoy their company when you see them, give yourself a 10 as well. If you spend half your life entertaining people you can't stand, or are feeling lonely, give yourself a 1. Otherwise, give yourself a score somewhere between the two.

- Now think about the time that you spend having fun. If your leisure time is filled with exciting hobbies and exotic holidays, give yourself a 10. If you have become such a workaholic that you feel guilty if you sit down for long enough to eat breakfast, give yourself a 1. Otherwise, give yourself an appropriate score between the two.

- Finally, think about what you do for others. If you spend at least 10 per cent of your time on fund-raising, charitable work or your

Maintaining the balance

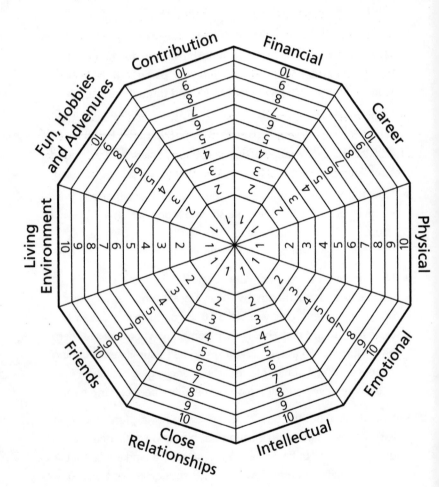

spiritual beliefs, give yourself a 10. If you can't remember the last time you did something for someone else without getting paid, give yourself a 1. If the truth lies somewhere between the two, give yourself the appropriate score.

- Once you have given yourself a score in each category, shade in the chart on page 122. This will give you a visual image of how well-balanced your life is currently. The 'ideal' decagon would have a score of 9 in all ten categories (it's never good to think any area of your life is perfect). What does your decagon look like? Which areas do you need to focus on?

This is an exercise that you can usefully repeat again and again. Many people do it once a year or whenever they feel that their lives have got a little out of balance. Happy people lead happy balanced lives, and the decagon is an excellent tool for checking that your life stays balanced.

CHAPTER 16

Living within your values

Let's suppose that your goal is to become a millionaire. One way of achieving that goal very quickly might be to set up a business selling crack cocaine.

I expect that suggestion makes you feel uncomfortable, but why does it do so? The answer, for the vast majority of people, is that selling drugs would contravene their values. If, in order to achieve your goal, you have to contravene your values, you will find that it won't bring you the fulfilment that would have come from achieving your success in a way that is more acceptable to you.

The crack-cocaine example is an extreme one. However, out in the real world, there are hundreds of thousands of examples of people who have compromised their values to achieve success in the eyes of the world and now find themselves unfulfilled by their achievements.

Values

Your values come from your innermost self. They reflect what matters most to you as a person. They might include:

- adventure
- contribution
- creativity
- duty
- friendship
- fun
- health
- independence
- integrity
- learning and growing
- love
- passion
- power
- security
- spirituality
- success
- variety

We arrange our values in a hierarchy and make decisions according to this hierarchy all the time without realising it.

Let me give you an example. Imagine a plank of wood across a mountain ravine. The plank is 6 inches wide and only 20 feet long, and the valley floor is more than 1,000 feet below. There are no handrails or other safety devices – if you lose your footing, you will die.

- Would you walk across the plank for £5?

- Would you walk across the plank for £500?

- Would you walk across the plank for £5,000?

- Would you walk across the plank for £500,000?

- Would you walk across the plank for £5,000,000?

- Would you walk across the plank for £500,000,000?

- Would you walk across the plank to gain your next promotion at work?

- Would you walk across the plank to get the medicine needed to avoid going blind?

- Would you walk across the plank to get the medicine your partner needed to avoid going blind?

- Would you walk across the plank to save your partner's life?

- Would you walk across the plank to save your child's life?

Your answers to these questions are determined by your sense of values. Most of us make these decisions subconsciously. I believe that your chances of living a happy, successful and fulfilling life will be increased enormously if you make these decisions *consciously*.

YOUR OWN VALUES

- Before you read any further, take some time to compile a list of your own top ten values, then rank them in order of importance. Choose from the ones listed on page 124 or add in a few more of your own. These core values are the very essence of your innermost self. Together they are your identity.

- Now take some more time to consider how well your current life meets these core needs. If your number-one value is friendship, is a career as a lighthouse keeper in the Outer Hebrides really likely to make you happy? If your number-one value is learning and growing, are you really going to be happy working on the cash till at the local supermarket?

No matter how successful you become in the eyes of others, you will never find true success unless you live within your own core values.

CHAPTER 17

Discarding the things that make you unhappy

However successful and fulfilling your life becomes, it is inevitable that you will still experience some moments of frustration and anger. However, there is probably a great deal more that you could do to keep these moments to a minimum.

Problems in the present

- Start by making a list of the top ten things that you 'have to put up with' at the moment. Some might be very minor things, like a washing machine that doesn't wash properly or a toaster that burns the toast every morning. Others might be more major things, like a client for whom you detest working or a friend who is making unreasonable demands on your time.

- Now look at each of these issues in the cold light of day and ask yourself honestly, do you really have to put up with them? A toaster that doesn't toast properly is not a big issue in its own right, but the irritation it causes grows exponentially with each burnt slice. You are worth more than that. You deserve a proper slice of toast in the morning. Take a decision now to do something about it. Dealing with little issues like this will make you feel tremendous.

Dealing with others

But what if the issue involves someone else? A negative friend, perhaps, who is draining your energy, or a family member who demoralises you with their constant criticism?

One way to deal with the problem might be to set some boundaries that you won't let anyone cross again. For example, you might decide that you won't work on a Sunday, or that you won't allow your mother to criticise you in front of others any longer, or that you won't accept your brother-in-law's swearing in front of your children. Boundaries are important because they let others know what you find acceptable. On so many occasions it turns out that the other person was completely unaware of the distress that their behaviour was causing you. Take some time now to make a list of any new boundaries that you would like to set and commit to a date to communicate them to the other party.

Another very useful way to improve your relationships is to learn to say no. If someone asks you to do something that you don't want to do, don't do it resentfully – say no, or, if you are put on the spot, make an excuse and say you'll get back to them.

Reading a book on assertiveness might also be of value to you. Assertiveness should not be confused with aggressiveness. An aggressive person seeks to get their own way by threats and intimidation and would not think twice about trampling on the rights of others in order to get their own way. An assertive person merely makes the other party aware of the consequences of their behaviour by focusing on the way that it makes them feel. For example, you might say, 'When you criticise me in front of my family it makes me feel like a small child again. I feel thoroughly demeaned and humiliated. I would like you to promise me that you won't do it again.'

But sometimes, with the best will in the world, you will have to accept that a relationship has run its course or has broken down beyond repair. Are there any relationships in your life that fall into this category? If so, then you have a decision to make. You can continue to allow this person to take up your time and sap the energy that you need to become the person you want to be, or you can take a painful decision to end a relationship that has outgrown its usefulness to both of you. It's often not an easy decision to make, but if you have stayed with me so far then I have absolute confidence that you will make the decision that is right for you.

Life is too short to put up with things that make you unhappy.

Problems from the past

A surprising number of outwardly successful people are unable to derive much satisfaction or fulfilment from their achievements because they are plagued by unresolved issues from the past. Common examples would include:

- anger at a former husband or wife
- regret over a bad investment decision
- guilt over having been unable to prevent a tragedy
- regret over not telling a parent something before they died

The event itself might date back 10, 20, 30 years or more, but that does not stop us ruminating over it:

- If only I had married someone else.
- If only I had not bought those shares.
- If only I had driven home another way that day.
- If only I had seen him one more time before he died.

You cannot let events from the distant past cast a shadow over your present life. So how can you stop yourself from doing it?

GUILT AND FORGIVENESS

If you are feeling guilty about something, try imagining that you are being accused of the offence in a court of law and write out your case for the defence. Setting the case out logically on paper can be a very effective way to prevent further rumination. Once you have persuaded yourself of your innocence, write a letter of forgiveness to yourself.

Even justifiable guilt can be dealt with in this way. If you made a mistake, write down what you think a fair punishment would be, then compare it with the sentence that you have already served. Shouldn't you have finished serving it years ago?

If you need to forgive someone else for something, try writing out their defence from their point of view. Another technique that works well here is to write a list of reasons for forgiving them and a list of reasons not to. This will usually make you realise the futility of continuing to harbour your resentment.

Many people find it helpful to write a brief letter of forgiveness to the other party. If they are no longer with us, write the letter anyhow, then burn it and scatter the ashes over their grave, or put it in a frame behind their photograph.

If these techniques do not work for you, you might consider investing in some professional counselling to help you to resolve your feelings about the issues that are troubling you. However successful you become in the future you will never feel truly fulfilled unless you are at peace with your past.

CHAPTER 18

Living by your rules

Let me start this chapter by asking you to take a few moments to answer three more questions:

- What would have to happen in order to make you feel really successful?

- What would have to happen in order to make you feel truly happy?

- What would have to happen in order for you to know for certain that someone loved you?

Now let me tell you something very, very important. Whatever you have just written is complete nonsense. The truth is that absolutely nothing has to happen in order for you to feel successful. You can feel successful any time you choose. So why don't you?

So very many people make the same mistake – they say, 'In order to feel successful I must earn £100,000 per year,' or 'I must have a million pounds in the bank,' or 'I must be able to afford a certain type of car.' And as a result, so many people who are hugely successful in the eyes of others spend their whole lives believing that they have failed. But who says so? Who makes up these stupid rules? Well, you do!

This is lunacy. You simply cannot go through your whole life saying, 'When I've got this amount of money in the bank then I'll be happy.' You can decide to be happy *now*. All you need to do is to change your rules.

Changing the rules

So how should you go about doing this?

- I'd like you to start by turning back to the hierarchy of values that you prepared in Chapter 16.

- Now go through each of your values in turn and write down what would have to happen for you to feel successful in this area. For example, if your number-one value is health and vitality, what would have to happen in order for you to feel really healthy – weigh 12 stone, run five miles every single day, have a 30-inch waist?

- Now look at each of these rules in the cold light of day and say to yourself, 'Who says so?' Where did these rules come from? Your parents, perhaps, your friends, your boss, the media? Or were they chosen entirely at random?

- Some of these things might be great goals to aim for one day in the future. But you don't have to feel miserable every day until you achieve them all. You can feel successful now. All you have to do is to invent some easier rules, for example:

  I feel healthy any time I:
  – run
  – swim
  – eat the right foods
  – climb a flight of stairs without getting breathless
  – feel 100 per cent alive

- Continue doing this with all your other values. Then instead of a set of rules that prevent you from feeling successful until months, possibly years, into the future, you have loads of different ways of feeling successful any time you choose to do so.

Make it as easy as you possibly can to feel successful. Success should be a journey, not a destination, and if you choose the right rules, you can enjoy every single step along the way.

CHAPTER 19

Enjoying the present moment

I have a lovely photograph on the wall of my home. It is of my twin daughters, aged about 22 months, playing in a water sprinkler one hot summer's day. They were absolutely fascinated by the jets of water: the way they caught the sunlight as they fell, the sensation as the water tumbled over their hands, the way that the water pressure changed when they put their fingers over the jets. They must have played in the sprinkler that day for two or three hours, and for the whole of that time they were totally absorbed in enjoying the present moment. That is how young children are. They are totally engrossed in whatever they are doing right now.

Then they grow up, and as they do so, they are bombarded by advice from adults. Advice like:

- Save it for a rainy day.

- Wait until you've grown up.

- It'll be worth it in the end.

And so we become conditioned to delay our gratification, until by the time we become adults, most of us have forgotten how to enjoy the present moment at all.

I found a lovely quotation about this in a book by the American author Dr Wayne Dyer. It goes:

First I was dying to finish high school and start college and then
I was dying to finish college and start working and then
I was dying to marry and have children and then
I was dying for my children to grow old enough for school so I
*   could return to work and then*
I was dying to retire and now
I am dying and suddenly I realise that I forgot to live.

Having goals to look forward to in the future is hugely important. However, unless you learn how to enjoy the present moment you will never get any real fulfilment from your achievements. And what is the point of being successful if you are not able to enjoy it? To my mind success without fulfilment is just another way to describe failure.

So how can you reverse a whole lifetime of conditioning and relearn how to live in the present moment? Well I believe that the key to this is to do three things.

Slow down

'Hurry up.'
'We're going to be late.'
'Get a move on.'

How many times each week does someone try to hurry you? We have to learn the habit of hurry in order to meet external deadlines. However, it's all too easy to internalise it to such an extent that our impatience starts to rule everything that we do.

Some activities have to be completed by a deadline. And there is benefit in doing some things as quickly as possible. But the pleasure that you could have got from so many other things will be totally denied to you if you try to do them too quickly. What is the point of rushing a country walk, a fine meal or making love to the person you adore?

Let children guide you

My second suggestion is that you allow children to guide you. If you don't have children yourself, try to spend some time with someone who has. Children, particularly very young children, have a natural ability to live totally in the present moment and we can learn a lot from living life at their pace for a few hours.

Try going on a country walk with a young child and let them set the pace. It's extraordinary how long they can spend examining a flower, a leaf, an earthworm or an insect. You'll see things that you haven't seen for years.

Ask the right questions

Finally, get into the habit of asking yourself the right questions. Questions like:

● How can I enjoy what I am doing right now?

● How can I make what I am doing more enjoyable?

● What is really great about my life right now?

Pleasure is great and you deserve to have as much of it in your life as possible. And you deserve to have it now, not tomorrow or next week or when you have achieved this or that or at any other time in the future, because the future by definition never arrives. Life is a series of present moments and each one needs to be lived to the full.

CHAPTER 20

Celebrating your successes

A few years ago I watched the end of the London Marathon. The atmosphere was electric. As each runner crossed the line, a battery of flashbulbs went off and the friends, relatives and medical staff stepped forward to hug the finishers and shower praise on them for their achievement.

Now imagine that you have just run a marathon. Imagine that you have just spent two or three or four or more hours running more than 26 miles. And imagine that as you rounded the last corner you found that no one was there to greet you. There was no finishing line, no cameras, no proud relatives, nothing but an empty street with not even a chalk line to mark the end of your achievement. How would that make you feel? Might it perhaps have just a little bit of an effect on how you felt about your achievement?

If this had happened to someone you knew, you would probably be outraged. 'How on earth could his family be so callous?' you might ask. 'My friend has run 26 miles and they couldn't even be bothered to be there to congratulate him on finishing!' Yet so many of us do this to ourselves all the time. We work for weeks, months, sometimes years trying to achieve something worthwhile, then one day we finally achieve it and we say to ourselves, 'Oh, that's good. What shall I attempt next?'

This is just so wrong. If you don't take the time to celebrate your achievements properly, then you will deny yourself much of the pleasure that should have been associated with them. And, if you don't make success a pleasurable experience for yourself, you will find that your motivation to achieve the next thing will be very significantly reduced.

In order to maintain both your long-term motivation and your sense of fulfilment, it is essential that you celebrate each of your successes in an appropriate way. For achieving a small milestone you might reward yourself with nothing more than some chocolates or a nice bottle of wine. For a major success you must think of something that is truly commensurate with the magnitude of your achievement.

This really does need to become an automatic part of your life. Even during an uneventful week you will usually be able to think of some success to celebrate if you go about it in the right way.

Once again this means asking yourself the right questions. These might include:

- What I am proud of achieving this week?
- What's great about my life right now?
- What am I grateful for in my life right now?

If you ask yourself the right questions, you will be able to find something to be proud of or grateful for even after the most difficult of weeks.

Keeping a journal

Finally I would urge you to get into the habit of keeping a journal to record all your best experiences. Whenever you experience a truly magical moment – the satisfaction of a major achievement, a moment of particular closeness with a loved one or just an especially enjoyable day out – write about how it made you feel in your journal. If you take a few minutes to capture the moment whilst it is still fresh in your mind, you will be able to relive it again and again whenever you want to in the future.

Over time your journal will become a priceless tool for making life into a virtuous circle. Each new achievement will improve your confidence and as your confidence in your ability grows, so will your ability to achieve even more. Until one day, perhaps, you find that you have truly become all that you are capable of being.

Back to the future

Before I close let me try to sum up what success means to me as succinctly as possible.

Success is not about money, status or those fleeting moments of perfect happiness that are so over over-exploited by advertisers. My definition of a successful person is as follows:

A successful person is someone who has a satisfactory present, a fully resolved past and a compelling, exciting and purpose-driven future.

Let me end this book by inviting you to join me in one last exercise that will bring the past, the present and the future together for you.

I'd like to invite you to return to that birthday party in ten years' time when all the people you care about most have gathered to make a speech to celebrate your life. Once again this is an exercise that needs to be read through in its entirety before you attempt it. In fact some people have even recorded the instructions on a cassette so that they are able to concentrate their whole attention on following them.

- I would like you to imagine that you are back in that glass time capsule again, the one that can take you ten years into the future. Close your eyes and imagine that it is taking you on through the rest of today, through the rest of this week, through the rest of the year and on and on until you reach that birthday party in ten years' time where all the people you care about most have gathered to pay tribute to your achievements. Get a picture firmly in your mind again of the four people whom you would most like to be there: someone from your work, your best friend, your partner and your mother, father or guardian, all looking as they will look in ten years' time.

- Each of these people is about to make a speech in celebration of all that you have achieved during the intervening ten years. And do you know what? You have achieved every single one of your goals. Every area of your life has become a triumph. Your financial affairs, your family life, your health, your emotional well-being, every aspect of your life is exactly as you would want it to be.

- How does it feel to have achieved so much? How does it feel to hear such glowing testimony to your achievements from the people you care about most?

- Stand as you would stand if you had already achieved all these things.

- Breathe as you would breathe if you had already achieved all these things.

- Say what you would say to yourself if you had already achieved all these things.

- See what you would see if you had already achieved all these things.

- Feel the way you would feel if you had already achieved so much.

- Then savour those feelings. This is what it feels like to live a life filled with passion and purpose, and when you've lived this way, for even a moment, you will never want to live any other way again.

You deserve a wonderful life. Make sure that you live every single moment of it to the full.

Further reading

I sincerely hope that my book will trigger a lifelong interest in personal development. If I have inspired you to read further, my top ten recommendations would be:

1. Stephen R. Covey, *The Seven Habits of Highly Effective People*, Simon and Schuster, 1989.

2. Anthony Robbins, *Awaken the Giant Within*, Simon and Schuster, 1991.

3. Wayne Dyer, *You'll See It When You Believe It*, Arrow, 1989.

4. Art Berg, *The Impossible Just Takes a Little Longer*, Piatkus Books, 2002.

5. Tony Buzan, *The Mind Map Book*, BBC Books, 1993.

6. Viktor Frankl, *Man's Search for Meaning*, Washington Square Press, 1985.

7. Ellen MacArthur, *Taking on the World*, Penguin, 2002.

8. Jack Canfield and Mark Victor Hanson, *Chicken Soup for the Soul*, Vermilion, 1993.

9. Richard Bandler, *Insider's Guide to Submodalities*, Meta Publications, 1993.

10. Martin Seligman, *Authentic Happiness*, Simon & Schuster, 2002.

How to contact the author

I hope you enjoyed this book. If you would like to book a place at one of our public seminars, or if your company would benefit from running the seminar in house, then visit us at:

www.whensuccessisnotenough.co.uk

Tell me about your achievements

I would love to hear about how this book has helped you. Email me your stories at *ajw@whensuccessisnotenough.co.uk*

Index